Ḥamīd al-Dīn al-Kirmānī

The Institute of Ismaili Studies
Ismaili Heritage Series, 3
General Editor: Farhad Daftary

Previously published titles:

Paul E. Walker, *Abū Ya'qūb al-Sijistānī: Intellectual Missionary* (1996)

Heinz Halm, *The Fatimids and their Traditions of Learning* (1997)

Ḥamīd al-Dīn al-Kirmānī

Ismaili Thought in the Age of al-Ḥākim

Paul E. Walker

I.B.Tauris
LONDON • NEW YORK
in association with
The Institute of Ismaili Studies
LONDON

Published in 1999 by
I.B.Tauris & Co Ltd
Victoria House
Bloomsbury Square
London WC1B 4DZ
175 Fifth Avenue
New York NY 10010

in association with
The Institute of Ismaili Studies
42–44 Grosvenor Gardens
London SW1W 0EB

In the United States of America
and in Canada distributed by
St Martin's Press
175 Fifth Avenue
New York NY 10010

A full CIP record for this book is available from the British Library
A full CIP record for this book is available from the Library of Congress

ISBN 1 85043 321 3
ISBN 1 85043 420 1

Library of Congress catalog card number: available

Typeset in ITC New Baskerville by Hepton Books, Oxford
Printed and bound in Great Britain by WBC Ltd, Bridgend

The Institute of Ismaili Studies

The Institute of Ismaili Studies was established in 1977 with the object of promoting scholarship and learning on Islam, in the historical as well as contemporary contexts, and a better understanding of its relationship with other societies and faiths.

The Institute's programmes encourage a perspective which is not confined to the theological and religious heritage of Islam, but seek to explore the relationship of religious ideas to broader dimensions of society and culture. They thus encourage an interdisciplinary approach to the materials of Islamic history and thought. Particular attention is also given to issues of modernity that arise as Muslims seek to relate their heritage to the contemporary situation.

Within the Islamic tradition, the Institute's programmes seek to promote research on those areas which have, to date, received relatively little attention from scholars. These include the intellectual and literary expressions of Shiʿism in general, and Ismailism in particular.

In the context of Islamic societies, the Institute's programmes are informed by the full range and diversity of cultures in which Islam is practised today, from the Middle East, Southern and Central Asia and Africa to the industrialized societies of the West, thus taking into consideration the variety of contexts which shape the ideals, beliefs and practices of the faith.

The publications of the Institute fall into several distinct categories:

1. Occasional papers or essays addressing broad themes of the relationship between religion and society in the historical as well as modern contexts, with special reference to Islam,

but encompassing, where appropriate, other faiths and cultures.

2. Proceedings of conferences or symposia.
3. Works exploring a specific theme or aspect of Islamic faith or culture, or the contribution of an individual figure or writer.
4. Translations of poetic or literary texts.
5. Editions or translations of significant texts of a primary or secondary nature.
6. Ismaili studies.

This book falls under the category six listed above.

In facilitating these and other publications, the Institute's sole aim is to encourage original, interesting and mature thought, scholarship and analysis of the relevant issues. There will naturally be a diversity of views, ideas and interpretations, and the opinions expressed, will be those of the authors.

Ismaili Heritage Series

A major Shi'i Muslim community, the Ismailis have had a long and eventful history. Scattered in many regions of the world, in Asia, Africa, and now also in the West, the Ismailis have elaborated diverse intellectual and literary traditions in different languages. On two occasions they had states of their own, the Fatimid caliphate and the Nizari state of Iran and Syria during the Alamut period. While pursuing particular religio-political aims, the leaders of these Ismaili states also variously encouraged intellectual, scientific, artistic and commercial activities.

Until recently, the Ismailis were studied and judged almost exclusively on the basis of the evidence collected or fabricated by their enemies, including the bulk of the medieval heresiographers and polemicists who were hostile towards the Shi'is in general and the Ismailis among them in particular. These authors in fact treated the Shi'i interpretations of Islam as expressions of heterodoxy or even heresy. As a result, a 'black legend' was gradually developed and put into circulation in the Muslim world to discredit the Ismailis and their interpretation of Islam. The Christian Crusaders and their occidental chroniclers, who remained almost completely ignorant of Islam and its internal divisions, disseminated their own myths of the Ismailis, which came to be accepted in the West as true descriptions of Ismaili teachings and practices. Modern orientalists, too, have studied the Ismailis on the basis of hostile sources and the fanciful occidental accounts of medieval times. Thus, legends and misconceptions have continued to surround the Ismailis through the twentieth century.

In more recent decades, however, the field of Ismaili studies has been revolutionized due to the recovery and study of genuine Ismaili sources on a large scale – manuscript materials which in different ways survived the mass destruction of the Fatimid and Nizari Ismaili libraries. These sources, representing diverse literary traditions produced in Arabic, Persian and Indic languages, had hitherto been secretly preserved in private collections in India, Central Asia, Iran, Afghanistan, Syria and the Yemen.

Modern progress in Ismaili studies has already necessitated a complete re-writing of the history of the Ismailis and their contributions to Islamic civilization. It has now become clear that the Ismailis founded important libraries and institutions of learning such as al-Azhar and the Dar al-'Ilm in Cairo, while some of their learned *da'is* or missionaries developed unique intellectual traditions amalgamating their theological doctrines with a diversity of philosophical traditions in complex metaphysical systems. The Ismaili patronage of learning and extension of hospitality to non-Ismaili scholars was maintained even in such difficult times as the Alamut period when the community was preoccupied with its survival in an extremely hostile milieu.

The Ismaili Heritage Series, published under the auspices of the Department of Academic Research and Publications of The Institute of Ismaili Studies, aims to make available to wide audiences the results of modern scholarship on the Ismailis and their rich intellectual and cultural heritage as well as certain aspects of their more recent history and achievements.

Contents

Preface xi

1 The Imam and the *Dāʿī* 1

2 The Works of al-Kirmānī 25

3 Al-Kirmānī and the *Daʿwa* 47

4 Double Observance by Works and Knowledge 62

5 God, Creation and the Cosmic Order 80

6 The City of God 104

Appendix A: Al-Kirmānī and the Philosophers 118
Appendix B: Al-Kirmānī's Citations of His Own Works 125
Appendix C: The Author's Table of Contents for the *Rāḥat al-ʿaql* 131

Notes 142
Bibliography 156
Index 161

Preface

The purpose of this book is to introduce a major Ismaili scholar and writer from the time of the Fatimid caliph-imam al-Ḥākim bi-Amr Allāh, who reigned from 386/996 until 411/1021, to English readers. Ḥamīd al-Dīn Abu'l-Ḥasan Aḥmad b. ʿAbdallāh al-Kirmānī, to use his full name, was so important in the *daʿwa* (the teaching and proselytizing organ of the Ismaili movement) of that era that he deserves recognition alone for his support and defence of his imam. Beyond that, however, al-Kirmānī possessed a profoundly ingenious theoretical mind, which allowed him both to master the philosophical and scientific achievement of the best Arabic works of his day and to express their principles in a way that made sense in terms of the instruction provided by the *daʿwa*. After writing numerous books and treatises which contain a fascinating mixture of religion and philosophy, he ultimately disappeared only to be remembered through them. The histories and chronicles are silent about him. In fact there is now no information about his life that does not come directly from his own words. Yet we know that he was the first of the great eastern Iranian *dāʿīs* to take up residence in Cairo, the capital of the Fatimids. And we are fairly certain that he was summoned there by al-Ḥākim's newly appointed head of the *daʿwa*. His scholarship was obviously impressive even then and his reputation grew afterwards. Much later Ismailis who looked back on that period tended to see it primarily in terms of al-Kirmānī's contributions. It is as if he defined the best of his age and was its permanent legacy. Although we now know a great deal more about the reign of al-Ḥākim and many of the events that took place during it in

Egypt and elsewhere, only some of which concerned al-Kirmānī, in the literature of thought and the sciences of this period, no other figure in the *da'wa* came even remotely close to him. It is thus certainly proper to regard him as its spokesman and his works as its finest achievement.

Had al-Kirmānī been merely an active agent of the Ismaili *da'wa* and not a writer of profoundly influential works of doctrine, he might have been more readily ignored. That he also contributed to and represented a scientific outlook which matches most closely the thought of his contemporary Ibn Sīnā, makes him doubly fascinating. But, ironically, modern scholarship has tended to note simply in passing his importance both as an outstanding *dā'ī* and a major theologian within the Islamic philosophical tradition. His greatest work, the *Rāḥat al-'aql*, was edited by two prominent Egyptian scholars, Muḥammad Kāmil Ḥusayn and Muḥammad Muṣṭafā Ḥilmī, and published as long ago as 1953 in Cairo by the Ismaili Society of Bombay (in conjunction with E. J. Brill). Its overwhelming complexity, sophistication and resulting difficulty were immediately recognized. Although as a result he gained some notice, he still attracted little serious scholarship. Despite the publication of more of his books and treatises in later years, few were willing to undertake the arduous task of deciphering, evaluating and ultimately explaining the workings of his mind as it appeared in his individual writings or in his thought as a whole.

This deplorable situation finally changed, and changed dramatically, with the publication of Daniel De Smet's *La Quiétude de l'intellect: Néoplatonisme et gnose ismaélienne dans l'oeuvre de Ḥamîd ad-Dîn al-Kirmânî (Xe/XIes.)* in 1995. Although De Smet had written a few short pieces on al-Kirmānī earlier, he now offered an extremely important, full-scale study of his philosophy and its context and sources. This book constituted, at last, a truly impressive contribution to the scholarly understanding of al-Kirmānī, one he had deserved but had not received. Nevertheless, much more can and should be said about him, although his works are not all in print and many of those that have been published have appeared with serious textual problems and flaws. There are as well quite interesting issues of interpretation regarding al-Kirmānī's thought and how to classify it. De Smet has both set an enviable scholarly standard for evaluating what al-Kirmānī said in his books and also, in the process, proposed ways to understand his thought that involve an interpretation which will in itself stimulate further investigation of him.

This book, however, is not the appropriate place to engage in the detail and nuance necessary for such scholarly debates. Al-Kirmānī remains largely unknown to the reader of English, and here my most pressing responsibility is to bring together the information about the man and his works, and to provide a guide to his thought in such a way that others – specialist and interested amateur alike – may follow and understand him. An exhaustive treatment has, therefore, been postponed in favour of an introduction and a preliminary accounting of the basic facts and ideas. Accordingly, the present book examines this great *dā'ī* as a member of the Ismaili *da'wa* and tries to explain his thought in broad terms. Its purpose is similar to my study, published in this same series, of al-Kirmānī's important predecessor, Abū Ya'qūb al-Sijistānī. Unfortunately, however, readers of that book will find that the approach required here is quite different. For al-Sijistānī a fair amount of previous scholarship already existed, much of it done by me. In his case, I was not only long familiar with the subject, but had established for him a base on which to build yet more. Since, for example, my earlier books and articles on al-Sijistānī contained a full apparatus of source citations, I decided that I could attempt a new interpretation of him without burdening the reader with a distracting array of notes and other academic niceties. For al-Kirmānī, however, this is simply not feasible. Much as I might wish to leap directly to that later, more advanced stage, there exists no foundation for it. And despite De Smet's valuable beginning, many references and details must be included to support my exposition. I have tried, nevertheless, to keep in mind twin obligations, one to the scholarly expert who will demand to know where I have found the information I relate, and the other to the less expert reader who wants to learn more about the era of al-Ḥākim and about his ardent supporter, the great *dāʿī* and philosophical theologian, al-Kirmānī, whose writings so brilliantly defined Ismaili thought in those momentous times nearly a millennium ago.

While writing this study I was helped by a number of colleagues and associates whom it is my pleasure to acknowledge and thank. Firstly, I owe a special debt of gratitude to Dr Farhad Daftary who responded positively to my offer to add a book on al-Kirmānī to this series and who shepherded it through to press. His comments and suggestions most certainly helped to improve the text at innumerable points. I also benefited from a careful reading of an earlier draft by Professor Zayn Kassam of Pomona College whose knowledge of the philosophical problems in Islamic, especially Ismaili, literature and whose sensitivity to the nuances of its language often kept my words within the bounds of intelligibility. At The Institute of Ismaili Studies in London, my typescript underwent an enviably thorough review and was skilfully edited in a way that rarely occurs these days. Among those who participated, I should like especially to thank Kutub Kassam who queried many of my vague or overly enthusiastic statements; his suggestions frequently compelled me to rethink a critical point and the final work is the better for it.

Here in Chicago, the assistance of Professor Farouk Mustafa, who was consulted on the rendering of some passages of al-Kirmānī's writings, was invaluable. Likewise Bruce Craig and his staff in the University of Chicago library provided much-needed support. Although many of the works cited here are printed and quite widely available, several exist only in manuscript. My sources in these cases were the Hamdani Collection, Tübingen University, the University of Bombay Library and The Institute of Ismaili Studies, and I must thank those who facilitated my access to copies of these texts.

P.E.W.

1

The Imam and the *Dāʿī*

Introduction

The reign of the Fatimid caliph al-Ḥākim bi-Amr Allāh was intensely personal and direct. More than possibly any of his predecessors in the century before and certainly after him, his imamate featured the involvement of its sovereign in all aspects of civil government and religious leadership. Coming to command at the early age of just sixteen, he struggled constantly to assert himself against an usurping army of bureaucrats who, quite naturally, sought to shield him and to exempt him of the responsibilities they felt appointed to shoulder in his stead. Yet he succeeded to the end in preserving his own individual access to an adoring public; his rule was broadly popular, and he himself never ceased to be acclaimed for both lavish generosity and an almost legendary ability to bring an awe-inspiring majesty wherever and whenever he appeared. After the era of the Prophet, there are few examples in Islamic history to match his; but while contemporaries noted the imam's exemplary intentions and his persistent attempts to correct and ameliorate the social and economic life of his subjects, they also recorded against him a long list of what they felt were wrong or aberrant actions. The elites often seemed particularly to suffer from his wrath and disdain; many of them lost their lives and possessions and it is their story that most concerned the historians and chroniclers. There were also, it is true, any number of baffling twists and turns in the progress of al-Ḥākim's rule. No simple description even comes close to it; too much happened that neither those who observed it nor those who wrote about it later could explain.[1]

But it was a time of great enthusiasm for the Ismaili understanding of Islam and for the *da'wa* that promoted and taught it. Al-Ḥākim himself was a rallying figure for the Shī'a everywhere; mobs in Baghdad might stage a demonstration calling out his name in preference to that of the Abbasid caliph. But there is in this picture a dichotomy: on the one hand, it features the personal image of the active imam who inspired a reverential and devoted following – a portrait seldom presented in the surviving documents; and at the same time, another, darker account which, at its worst, foists on the imam the authorship of incredulously maniacal edicts and laws and, at its best, simply expresses wonder and astonishment, as if the events in question defy an acceptable explanation, as if they had never been witnessed before and would not occur again. It is no accident, nor is it through malice alone that later ages hardly knew what to make of the records left to them from this singular era.

The problem of properly understanding or appreciating the reign of al-Ḥākim was not merely a dilemma for non-Ismailis, whose normal hostility to an Ismaili ruler would have contributed to the darkening of any account of his activities. It also deeply affected those most loyal to the imam, a fact that is shown clearly in contemporary treatises. Like any bureaucracy, the *da'wa* had expected to assume an intermediate role between the imam who led them with unerring and divinely sanctioned guidance and the ordinary believers they were sworn to instruct and counsel. It is very clear, however, that even ardent supporters of the imam found the situation troubling because they could not comprehend his leadership in the way that they were formerly accustomed. The *dā'īs* tended, of course, to infer their own authority, but they discovered in this particular case that their imam would not accede to their desires. He would not be controlled by them any more than by the administrators of his empire, its army, the scholars and the elites or even, for that matter, the ordinary people of his realm. Al-Ḥākim, whatever else might be said of him, was arguably the ruler least dependent and least subservient to his own advisers, subordinates, servants and followers.

For this period two richly detailed contemporary accounts exist, both written by observers who resided, at least a part of the time, in Egypt. One, the *History* of Yaḥyā of Antioch, was written by a Christian with some personal access to the elite members of al-Ḥākim's inner circle until he left for Antioch in the year 404/1013. The other is by a non-Ismaili amir, al-Musabbiḥī, who was certainly himself an insider who could and did converse with the caliph in person on occasion. The latter account is for the most part unfortunately lost except for quotations that appear in the writings of later historians. Although extremely valuable and in fact indispensable, neither of these sources, understandably, offers a complete or even an accurate account of the workings of the Ismaili *daʿwa* or of the religious dimension behind al-Ḥākim's policies and pronouncements.[2]

For such information it is necessary to turn to the records of the *daʿwa* itself which, however, tend to be elusive because of the secrecy involved in its work, most especially for activities and attitudes outside the domain of the Fatimids. Still, centuries later when the 9th/15th-century Ṭayyibī historian Idrīs ʿImād al-Dīn composed his *ʿUyūn al-akhbār*[3] – a comprehensive history of the Ismaili imams – for his account of al-Ḥākim's reign he could find a number of important proclamations from the time as well as, most significantly, the works of the contemporary *dāʿī* Ḥamīd al-Dīn al-Kirmānī who, more than any other representative of the *daʿwa*, epitomized, at least in the estimation of Idrīs, the great achievements of that age.

Al-Kirmānī was a forceful, intellectually gifted apologist for al-Ḥākim, one who never failed to advocate and defend his imamate, whether to wavering and deviant members of the *daʿwa* or to the establishment behind the Buyids or Ithnā ʿasharī Shīʿa of Abbasid Iraq. In addition al-Kirmānī, whose scholarly accomplishments and knowledge were a match for any of his contemporaries, including possibly the philosopher Ibn Sīnā, actually played an important role in Egypt, at the very capital of the empire, during a difficult and troubling moment in the final years of al-Ḥākim's reign. All in all, Idrīs may be right in his assessment; the era of al-Ḥākim and of his erudite champion, al-Kirmānī, belong together. In our surviving records, where much of the information, however specific and detailed it may be, reflects uncertainty, puzzlement, or outright hostility, the writings of al-Kirmānī, who was also an eye-witness and who appreciated better than others the religious aspect of what he saw and what he was commissioned to teach, is from the Ismaili perspective a major source, perhaps the defining source, for the age as a whole.

A Crisis in the Da'wa and the Arrival of al-Kirmānī

For the Fatimids, religion and state were never separate. The religious appeal of the Ismaili *da'wa* was intrinsically linked to the imamate and thus also to the caliphate of the reigning imam. In practice, in part because it was the pattern developed under his father and grandfather, al-Ḥākim delegated two key functions to one person: that of the *da'wa,* as represented in the position of the chief *dā'ī,* the *dā'ī al-du'āt,* and that of the judiciary in the office of chief judge, the *qāḍī al-quḍāt.*[4] Accordingly, these two aspects of Fatimid rule were merged in one office. The chief judge had to hold court and preside over the legal affairs of the empire. At the same time, as chief *dā'ī,* he directed the teaching programme and propagation of the *da'wa,* here entailing, at a minimum, his personal appearance to read lessons to the faithful during the weekly 'sessions of wisdom' (*majālis al-ḥikma*) which were sometimes, of necessity, repeated for two or more different audiences in the same week. In addition, in contrast to his office as chief judge, as chief *dā'ī* he presided over a much larger domain since the *da'wa* extended in theory, and probably in actuality, to all the territories of Islam, even to areas controlled by enemies of the Fatimids.

From the beginning of al-Ḥākim's reign, this combined office was occupied by sons and grandsons of the great Qāḍī al-

Nuʿmān (d. 363/974), whose books and treatises formed the standard curriculum and the source material for the study of Ismaili law, as well as the written history of Fatimid rule itself. It is quite likely that Ismaili law, as opposed to other matters of doctrine such as theology was, in the minds of these men, of paramount importance for the ongoing activities of the *daʿwa*. Their work as judges in the *qāḍī*'s court and as teachers or preachers in the weekly *majālis al-ḥikma*, where Ismaili doctrine was taught, were therefore compatible since their respective roles were not completely dissimilar. For them, what they taught to an audience of the Ismailis also involved aspects of the law or an interpretation of it.

Even after the imam had deposed and executed several members of this family of *qāḍīs* – for reasons we understand only dimly, but which may have involved corruption of various kinds – and had thereby interrupted the hold on this office of the Qāḍī al-Nuʿmān's clan, he appointed another experienced Ismaili jurist, al-Fāriqī, to the same dual role. Al-Fāriqī, in fact, vigorously attempted to uphold both responsibilities. Not only did he hold court in Fustat, the older city, but he conducted as many as five *majālis*[5] per week as *dāʿī*, and these sessions met only in the new capital of Cairo. The historians of the time remarked on the fervour of the population who responded to the *majālis al-ḥikma* with enthusiasm. Attendance at these gatherings grew and the Ismaili message – with its attendant devotion to al-Ḥākim, as imam – was apparently widely and favourably received.

Despite this policy and the seeming success of the various chief *qāḍīs*/*dāʿīs* in promoting Ismailism, on several occasions the imam expressed dissatisfaction both with the *daʿwa* – as administered by these men – and their conduct of public business. The most serious instances led in each case to dismissal. As with other examples of such action it is, given the paucity of our information, almost impossible to explain now what happened and why. However, on the basis of certain hints in the sources, one might speculate that the men in question tried, as some others did in similar circumstances, to carve out their own independent spheres of influence or to join with another person who had that goal in mind. According to this interpretation, the imam might well have regarded such acts as disloyal and rebellious and their perpetrators as treasonous. There was, moreover, always a serious tension between the caliph and the representatives of powerful families such as those of al-Fāriqī, al-Nu'mān, Jawhar and others. Still, these are speculations.[6] More to the point are the steps actually taken by al-Ḥākim subsequent to these crises, especially in response to the last of them – the end of al-Fāriqī's tenure as *qāḍī al-quḍāt* and *dā'ī al-du'āt.*

The imam had closed the *majālis al-ḥikma* several times before his final dissatisfaction with al-Fāriqī, but on each occasion the sessions were eventually resumed. Late in Ramaḍān of 404/1014, however, he stopped the *majālis al-ḥikma* yet again. We cannot be sure exactly why, but a few months later he deposed al-Fāriqī and ordered his execution. Whether he was displeased with the way the 'sessions' were conducted or specifically with al-Fāriqī himself, or both, is hard to determine. Al-Fāriqī's crime, however, was obviously serious.

At this point in his rule, the imam faced more and more the paradox posed on the one hand by his popularity and on the other by a growing weariness with the constant demands it imposed on him and the attendant constraints which tended to restrict his personal freedom. He had by then put aside the normal extravagant regalia of his office and adopted a plain style of adornment, and he rode a donkey during his public outings surrounded by only a few grooms and retainers. Nevertheless, his outings increased, many by night, but also, for example, in the years 403/1013 and 404/1014, during Ramaḍān, he insisted on riding to each of the four congregational mosques on successive Fridays to pray with the people. As he rode out from the palace and back, he stopped frequently to receive petitions and to speak with the populace. On one such Friday in 404, he spent so much time talking and laughing with ordinary people that it took him all afternoon to return to the palace, even though it was only a short distance from the mosque.

But his desire to be accessible was clearly in conflict with the preservation of his independence. About this time he tried to appoint his cousin ʿAbd al-Raḥīm b. Ilyās as his heir apparent, perhaps in the hope that the latter would absorb some of the heavy demands on his own time and energy. At one point he decreed, for example, that all petitions be presented to either this cousin or to the *qāḍī* al-Fāriqī instead of to himself. This measure apparently did not bring the relief he sought and soon after he disposed of al-Fāriqī, while also deposing several key officers of the government and shutting down the *majālis al-ḥikma.*

For a time thereafter, al-Ḥākim attempted to govern in person without either a chief *qāḍī* or a chief *dāʿī* and without intermediaries of any kind other than his palace servants, a situation even more at odds with his evident desire to be free of incessant public responsibilities. Most critical under the circumstances was the office of chief *qāḍī*, a position that could not be left vacant for long. However, it was almost four months before he made an appointment to the post. During this time he consulted those he trusted most, among them Abu'l-Faḍl Jaʿfar, a blind scholar of grammar and lexicography to whom he had given the title 'Scholar of Scholars' (*ʿālim al-ʿulamāʾ*) and appointed to teach in the Dār al-ʿIlm, an academy he had established a decade earlier.[7] Abu'l-Faḍl Jaʿfar recommended that the best candidate for the office of chief *qāḍī* was Ibn Abi'l-ʿAwwām, a Ḥanbalī jurist with long experience in the Egyptian judiciary. The imam responded positively to this suggestion even though Ibn Abi'l-ʿAwwām was not an Ismaili. With this appointment – which was successful enough to last well into the next reign – the office of the chief judge was now occupied by someone unqualified and disinclined to assume responsibility for the *daʿwa.* With respect to the law, however, the imam stipulated that four Ismaili legal experts should sit in the court with this Ḥanbalī chief judge to cover those cases that might be presented where Ismaili law should prevail. The *daʿwa* would require a different solution and it could certainly no longer be intrinsically linked to the administration of, or even possibly the study of, law.

For the *da'wa* al-Ḥākim chose an old and trusted aide, a man imprecisely known by the name Abū Manṣūr Khatkīn the Ḍayf, who also bore the *nisba* al-'Aḍudī, earned from previous service to the Buyid amir 'Aḍud al-Dawla. Unlike his predecessors, Khatkīn did not come from the judiciary. He had once briefly been Fatimid governor of Damascus and he was said to know Syria well both from the direct experience he had accumulated there and from handling the imam's correspondence with the province. During the famous incident that led to the destruction of the Church of the Holy Sepulchre in Jerusalem, it was this same Khatkīn who first brought to al-Ḥākim's attention the fraud practised in it. Still later, when the imam dispatched agents to open the house of the early Shī'ī imam Ja'far al-Ṣādiq (d. 148/765) in Madina and retrieve its contents, he put the whole operation under the supervision of this man. From these details and others, a picture emerges of Khatkīn as a man who was a fully capable and an undeniably devoted servant. In any case, once al-Ḥākim had separated the *da'wa* from the judiciary, it was Khatkīn who assumed the former responsibility and finally, after an interruption of several months, the *majālis al-ḥikma* were restored, possibly at the end of 405/1015 or more likely at the beginning of 406/1015.

The reconstituting of the local *da'wa* – that is, in the capital (there is no obvious sign that the *da'wa* abroad had stopped or been interrupted) – therefore commenced at this time and a major step in the process involved the arrival of al-Kirmānī in Cairo. It is very likely that Khatkīn himself was responsible for al-Kirmānī's presence there, and that he had even summoned him with this very purpose in mind. But there is almost no way to know what was in the mind of al-Ḥākim or of his new chief *dā'ī*. The information in our histories, especially that coming from the massive chronicle of al-Musabbiḥī, begins to dry up at the end of 405. Yaḥyā reports a few precious facts from later years, but in general the final years of al-Ḥākim, from 406 to 411, are not adequately covered. Under these circumstances, it is especially significant that al-Kirmānī himself provides what constitutes crucial eye-witness information, albeit not with the intention of recording or preserving history.

By 405/1014 al-Kirmānī was most certainly already a respected and well recognized author of Ismaili works and a ranking authority in the external *daʿwa.* His previous writings in defence of al-Ḥākim's imamate must have been appreciated in Cairo. After his arrival in the capital, he wrote yet another strong defence of this imamate and for the eventual continuation of the Fatimid line for generations to come. This treatise he called 'Happy Tidings of the Good News' (*Mabāsim al-bishārāt*). In it, most importantly, he unashamedly confesses to the dismay and confusion he observed within the *daʿwa* in Egypt; quite clearly he had only recently arrived. His words are the only direct evidence of how the Egyptian Ismailis had reacted to what was happening there. The year of al-Kirmānī's arrival was either 405 or 406 (1014 or 1015), as noted by an indirect reference in the treatise itself which, however, has been given by copyists as either one or the other with no exact way to determine, at the moment, which reading is correct. Nevertheless, al-Kirmānī also wrote at about the same time another work, a short epistle called the 'Glittering Treatise on the Meaning of Tawḥīd' (*al-Risāla al-durriyya fī maʿnā al-tawḥīd*). At the beginning of this, he explicitly recognizes the important role of Khatkīn, whom he calls 'the Door [*bāb*] to the imam's mercy, who bears the title *al-ṣādiq al-ma'mūn* and is the *dāʿī al-duʿāt.*' Clearly, then, al-Kirmānī was, when he composed this treatise, working under the supervision of Khatkīn. Moreover, the title *al-ṣādiq al-ma'mūn* (the Truly Reliable) was, according to Yaḥyā, granted to Khatkīn by al-Ḥākim after he was first appointed chief *dāʿī.* Thus al-Kirmānī's testimony indicates his involvement in Cairo at this specific time and his treatise, accordingly, reflects the doctrinal message of the *daʿwa* in this particular period, that is, about 406/1015 to 408/1017.

Al-Kirmānī's Previous Career in the Eastern Provinces and Buyid Iraq

As there is no trace of al-Kirmānī in any of the histories and other records, either of his activities in Cairo or his previous career in the east, when his own words refer to a detail of his personal life they assume extraordinary value. An assessment of such passages is necessary, moreover, not just for an account of the momentous events in Cairo just mentioned, but even more so for al-Kirmānī's earlier positions. There is simply no other information about him or his role in the *da'wa*. Even the later Ṭayyibī authorities, such as the historian Idrīs, probably depend exclusively on al-Kirmānī's own comments found here and there in his writings.

Ṭayyibī authorities such as Idrīs state that al-Kirmānī had the title '*Ḥujja* of the Two Iraqs' (*Ḥujjat al-'Irāqayn*) – i.e., Iraq proper and parts of Persia. If he held the rank of *ḥujja*, that would make him the director of the *da'wa* in his region and its highest local authority. There seems to be no valid reason to reject this usage since it fits with the other information about al-Kirmānī and is unlikely to have been arbitrarily invented by later writers. It is clear that he held a high rank in the *da'wa*, for otherwise he would not have presumed to write the kinds of treatises he did. Furthermore, the very fact of their preservation by the *da'wa* attests to their, and therefore his own, importance. Al-Kirmānī's *nisba* connects him to the province of Kirmān; but other references strongly suggest that, although he may have come from Kirmān and even retained control over its local *da'wa*, his main centre of activity was Iraq and specifically Baghdad, the Abbasid capital. According to his own testimony, his most ambitious book, the 'Comfort of Reason' (*Rāḥat al-'aql*) received its final revision in Iraq in the year 411/1020. Another title mentioned by al-Kirmānī as his own, *al-Majālis al-Baghdādiyya wa'l-Baṣriyya* (The Baghdādī and Baṣran Lectures), indicates that he must have spent time in both these cities and that he had delivered a series of lectures to the *da'wa*, and perhaps others, in each. To cite another example of this kind of information, at one point in a treatise of his known as *al-Waḍī'a fī maʿālim al-dīn,* he happens to mention a certain weight used in Madina. To explain its value he chooses the equivalent *Baghdādī raṭl.*[8] In yet other works he cites 'orders that arrived from the Sublime Presence,' 'a decree to the leaders of the *daʿwa* in the east,' 'a decree sent to Fars,' and there is even his own epistle which was written in Fustat but intended for a subordinate of his in Jīruft in the province of Kirmān.

More telling evidence of al-Kirmānī's involvement in the Irāqī and Baghdādī sphere is his treatise 'The Lamps that Establish the Imamate' (*al-Maṣābīḥ fī ithbāt al-imāma*) which he wrote specifically as an attempt to win over to the Ismaili cause the Buyid vizier of Iraq, Fakhr al-Mulk. This man, Abū Ghālib 'Alī b. Muḥammad b. Khalaf, was appointed vizier by Bahā' al-Dawla, the Buyid amir, in 401/1011, and he thereafter governed Baghdad until his own death early in 407/1016. His charge, moreover, was specifically Iraq, and not Fars or Kirmān which were controlled by others. Like most of the Buyids and their appointees, Fakhr al-Mulk was Shīʿī, as is clear from his extremely close alliance with the heads (*naqīb, nuqabā'*) of the *ashrāf.*[9] Sharīf al-Murtaḍā, for example, the leader of the Irāqī *ashrāf* and an important Twelver scholar, eulogized him upon his death and he was buried at the shrine of 'Alī at Najaf.[10]

Al-Kirmānī thus appeals in this treatise to a convinced Shīʿī who might be presumed to have already accepted the concept of an 'Alid imamate. Nevertheless, the situation must have been difficult since al-Kirmānī's own imam was al-Ḥākim bi-Amr Allāh, the caliph and ruler of a rival territory. The opening words of address in this treatise are thus especially interesting and remarkable, and it is obviously necessary to read into them a message that lies between the lines. Here is what al-Kirmānī says:

> Now then: when I observed the lord of the mighty and ornament of the leading and honourable ministers, commander of the noble armies, Fakhr al-Mulk, the *wazīr* of all *wazīrs* – may

God prolong his life – being endowed by God with particular intelligence and understanding, granted knowledge and perception, crowned with the nobility of prophetic guardianship, made infallible through 'Alid infallibility, and professing devotion through the love of the pure family – the family of *Taha* and *Yasin*[11] – I imagined further that one of the satans who intimate in the hearts of the people, one of the abominable devils, had assumed a lofty station in his council and reported to him some notions that produced in him an obstacle to the way of God and an insolence toward God, a breaking away from obedience to God, and denying God's signs. And besides there is in his service nobody induced to make known what reaches him of the materials that constitutes the blessings that emanate from the Saints of Felicity, the Lords of the Community, to whom God enjoins obedience – may God keep them, past and present – and in particular the one of them among us, the current ruler. At that, deep concern for the faith and the truth of devotion and conviction and a judgment regarding what I ascribe to in the matter of God as being true belief, and the judgement of what *jihād* God has imposed on me in order to follow His way, provoked me to establish firmly the necessity of the imamate and prove truthful its being located in the family of *Taha* and *Yasin* among the imams – may God grant them benediction and peace – and most especially the correctness of the imamate of the one among them who occupies it in our own time, our master, the Commander of the Faithful, the Servant of God and His friend, al-Manṣūr Abū 'Alī al-Ḥākim bi-Amr Allāh – may God keep him and all the imams. The obligation to obey him and adhere to him is a consequence of the slight measure of their radiance that was communicated to me. Accordingly, I will produce brilliant proofs for it that defy refutation and evidence that withstands subversion. All this I put into a book in order to make him understand and apprehend through it the correctness of that most noble doctrine and belief, and that there be conceived in him an inclination in favour of the people of obedience to the extent that the bounty of God provides them support. I have done exactly that and called it the book of 'The Lamps that Establish the Imamate' which belong to the Master of the Age, on whom be peace, since what it contains in the way of proofs resembles the lamps that are like 'the things to throw at satans.'[12]

It is worth quoting this statement at length in part because it has not been noticed previously by scholars and in part because it suggests a great deal about the situation that al-Kirmānī and the Fatimids faced in Iraq. What makes the effort to understand the possible relationship between Fakhr al-Mulk and al-Kirmānī even more interesting is that this vizier's son Abū Shujā' Muḥammad al-Ashraf b. Muḥammad, was later to become vizier to the Fatimid imam al-Mustanṣir in Egypt.[13]

Al-Kirmānī's words clearly appeal to Fakhr al-Mulk's own devotion to Shī'ism, a fact evidently of common knowledge in Iraq. Indeed the Buyids as a whole were understood to be Shī'ī and thus their continued support of, or at the least tolerance for, the Abbasid caliphs seems anomalous, especially for the caliph al-Qādir who was put in office in the year 381/991 in place of al-Ṭa'i', whom the amir Bahā' al-Dawla had seen fit to depose. Over his long reign lasting until 422/1031, al-Qādir grew increasingly independent and more and more ardently Sunnī. Earlier on, he conceived a virulent hostility and hatred for the Fatimids. When al-Kirmānī noted in one of his treatises that the two great enemies of al-Ḥākim were 'Aḥmad' and 'Maḥmūd,' he was explicitly pointing to al-Qādir and to Maḥmūd of Ghazna respectively, both of whom were dangerously anti-Ismaili.[14]

But, if the Buyids were Shī'ī, why preserve the Abbasid caliphate at all? One sure answer is that to abolish the existing caliphate would have been difficult, if not impossible, without substituting another. By allowing the Abbasids to continue under a fairly tight rein, the Buyids were able to maintain their own independence. The Buyids were, in addition, originally Zaydī; they had no manifest reason therefore to accept or even possibly to sympathize with the Ismaili imams. Moreover, the amir 'Aḍud al-Dawla, who apparently began his rule in Iraq without any policy of overt hostility to the Fatimids, later began to express it. He saw himself in grand, imperial terms as a sovereign even greater than the caliphs. To enhance his royal majesty, he assumed various pre-Islamic emblems of kingship. At one point, the Fatimid caliph al-ʿAzīz dispatched men from Cairo who succeeded in removing one such royal emblem, the silver lion figure on the prow of ʿAḍud al-Dawla's personal river craft, and bringing it back to Egypt.[15] Although it delivered a blow to the amir's overreaching pride, this incident, like others, reveals a growing animosity. The rivalry was less religious than political, but the two sides became and remained enemies, mutual adherence to Shīʿism notwithstanding.

The Iraqi countryside was another matter. Many of the tribal groups there were Shīʿī and were also quite susceptible to the appeal of the Ismaili *daʿwa*. ʿAlī b. Mazyad and the Mazyadids, centred around al-Ḥilla, were Shīʿī in general and frequently expressed their support of the Fatimids. In any case they could be counted on as a refuge for city dwellers fleeing from the regularly occurring Sunnī–Shīʿī riots and other disturbances in the major towns, particularly in Baghdad. Another group under Qirwāsh b. al-Muqallad likewise could and did announce for the Fatimids. At one critical juncture in 401/1010, this tribal leader declared for al-Ḥākim and pronounced the Friday *khuṭba* in his name. Thus, for that moment, much of the rural Iraqī heartland belonged to the Fatimids. Already a Shīʿī mob in Baghdad had, during an incident in 398/1008, informally declared its inclination by shouting in the streets of the capital, 'Yā Ḥākim, yā Manṣūr.'[16]

The Abbasid caliph al-Qādir was sufficiently alarmed that he promptly began to orchestrate an increasingly vigorous response. Against the revolt of Qirwash, he asked the famous Ashʿarite theologian and Mālikī *qāḍī* al-Bāqillānī to intercede with the Buyid authorities in an attempt to undo the damage as quickly as possible.[17] In short order a threat of military action forced Qirwāsh to renounce his allegiance to the Fatimids. In the following year, during the vizierate of the same Fakhr al-Mulk, al-Qādir obtained from the local leaders of various factions, among them the major figures of the Twelver Shīʿīs and the *ashrāf* nobility, a proclamation and manifesto denouncing as bogus the Fatimid lineage of the Ismaili imams.

He also prompted one of the leading Muʿtazilīs of Iraq, al-Iṣṭakhrī, to compose a refutation of Ismaili doctrine.[18] Presumably, despite his Shīʿism, Fakhr al-Mulk acquiesced in many of the measures taken by the Abbasid caliph against the supporters of al-Ḥākim and the Ismailis. Al-Kirmānī perhaps alludes to this in his comment about a 'satan' in the vizier's council, by whom he can have meant the Abbasid caliph, or more plausibly any of several others such as the head of the local *ashrāf*.

Having lived through them, al-Kirmānī surely witnessed many of these events and probably observed them within Iraq and, in all likelihood in Baghdad itself. He thus knew well the vicissitudes of the local Shīʿī community and its struggle for recognition or ascendancy against various forces of Sunnism. This was the period just prior to his going to Cairo. He can only have written his 'The Lamps that Establish the Imamate' between about 402/1011 and 405 or 406/1015. The time is most likely to have been close to 404 because of fairly explicit references in the treatise to certain actions and policies of al-Ḥākim that may be dated to those years. May we therefore speculate that in sending such a forthright defence of al-Ḥākim's imamate to the Buyid vizier, he risked exposure, condemnation, and loss of life? Or did he have some local protection? The latter option seems less likely, although secrecy and outward dissimulation would have afforded the only sure protection without it.

Nevertheless, Baghdad was, during these years, the residence of important figures from a surprising variety of intellectual persuasions. The head of the *ashrāf* until his death in 406 was Sharīf al-Raḍī and he was followed by his brother Sharīf al-Murtaḍā, both noted scholars and Twelver Shīʿī authorities. Even more important, however, was the famous theologian and jurisprudent Shaykh al-Mufīd who taught there between occasional periods of exile caused by sectarian troubles. Al-Mufīd is credited with a work which, by its title, indicates that it is a response to a certain al-Kirmānī about the superiority of the Prophet Muḥammad over the rest of the prophets.[19] This al-

Kirmānī need not be our al-Kirmānī, but it is interesting that both al-Mufīd and the Ismaili *dā'ī* were active in Baghdad at the same time. In one of his treatises, the latter inserts an account of a debate he held with a Mu'tazilī on the question of the imamate. The writings of both al-Mufīd and al-Kirmānī show the influence of Mu'tazilī thought – especially those of al-Mufīd – though neither one would have been referred to by this term. Al-Kirmānī does not say where the debate occurred and he does not name his opponent. There were, in fact, many prominent Mu'tazilīs in Baghdad at that time. However, the most famous of them probably then lived elsewhere – namely 'Abd al-Jabbār – against whom al-Kirmānī wrote a refutation in a work he called *al-Naqḍ wa'l-ilzām* ('Criticizing and Consequence'), a treatise which was unfortunately lost long ago.

Al-Kirmānī's Role after his Arrival in Cairo

Having departed from Iraq, where he certainly knew that his enemies were numerous and all around, even if some among them, either openly or in secret, preserved a profound devotion to Shī'ism, al-Kirmānī had every right to anticipate a warm reception in the Cairo of his imam, al-Ḥākim. The city was after all the seat of the only ruling Shī'ī sovereign since 'Alī b. Abī Ṭālib, the Prophet's cousin and later successor. It was therefore genuinely the capital of prophetic authority and of 'Alid loyalty, in contrast to Baghdad which, despite the pro-Shī'ī leanings of the Buyids and their vizier Fakhr al-Mulk, was still dominated by non-Shī'ī *'ulamā'* and by the Sunnism of the Abbasid caliph. Going to the centre of the *da'wa* would surely allow him to breath freely. But, instead, to his consternation, the Fatimid domain was at the time afflicted by another sort of trouble, one not caused by lack of dedication, but ironically and in all likelihood by the opposite, an excess of it. Al-Kirmānī obviously arrived at a moment of deep uncertainty and no little despair; the Ismaili *da'wa* in Egypt clearly needed his help, rather, it would seem, than he theirs.

From other sources we have learned that al-Ḥākim had recently shut down the *majālis al-ḥikma* and temporarily interrupted the system by which the *daʿwa* in Egypt provided contact and instruction to ordinary members of the Ismaili community there. No evidence exists to suggest that the reason was more profound than the imam's dissatisfaction with the previous head of the *daʿwa*, al-Fāriqī; but there may have been more at stake, possibly that he found its earlier teachings unacceptable or its direction and control of affairs ineffective, and perhaps also corrupt. The only inside testimony, but obviously the most trustworthy, is the following highly important passage of the *Mabāsim* in which al-Kirmānī speaks rather bluntly about the situation that awaited him in Cairo.

> When as an immigrant [*muhājir*] I reached the Prophetic Presence, a pilgrim having come to the ʿAlid Seat, I beheld there a sky that had become dark with pervasive clouds, the people under the weight of a great tribulation, the observance of previous practices had been cancelled, and the faithful saints were kept from what they had earned. The practice of holding the Sessions of Wisdom [*majlis al-ḥikma*], which had provided them such a dividend of benefits, had been abandoned. The high among them were humbled; the low were on the rise. I observed that the saints of the rightly guiding *daʿwa* – may God spread far and wide their lights – and those most steeped in the defence of the imamate and most loyal to it had become confused by what had befallen them of such matters as to put premature gray in the temples, and they were overwhelmed by the repetition of such conditions which rightly ought to destroy none but the perpetrators of hypocrisy and rebellion. They were then in the throes of causing agitation one upon the other, each person accusing his associate of deviation and violations. Evil thoughts were playing tricks on them and malicious insinuations circulated among them. Thus they could not perceive what plain smoke had covered them nor what obvious trials afflicted them. As a result some entered upon a course of extremism and ascended even to its uppermost limit. Some turned away from religion and abandoned the preservation of the faith and its bonds. A few even overturned the very pillars of their belief and what they had once accepted freely and

willingly, having come to the brink of dissolution and disorder with necks outstretched to the misappropriation of the two-horned devils, their ardour in searching for true belief frustrated. Among them it is only individuals who approve by themselves of themselves for their spirits escaped by being reconciled in the words of God, 'He who is astray cannot harm you if you are properly guided.' [5: 105]

A superabundance of concern for the faith prompted in me a desire to save these suffering brethren – except for those who had so corrupted their being with a transformed doctrine that their very elements were inverted because their own hearts had imbibed the water of change, and they had become like burnt silver which no art can restore to its silverness or to its original state – by a regimen of effort and obedience that might fortify their hearts and put resolve back in their steps. [To accomplish this purpose I offer the following] clear affidavit of the imamate of the Imam al-Ḥākim bi-Amr Allāh, Commander of the Believers, and of its true reality ... [20]

From this opening declaration, al-Kirmānī proceeded to outline a complete endorsement for and defence of the imam and the imamate. Unlike his previous writings of the kind, however, it is evident that here he is speaking to members of the Ismaili community, especially to those who have wavered and strayed from the accepted doctrine. He is attempting to bring order and calm back into the *da'wa.*

Surely he wrote this treatise with official blessing, although it does not explicitly credit any one but the imam. A note at the end states, however, that it was dictated to the *mu'adhdhin* of the al-Azhar mosque. Moreover, the next work of al-Kirmānī, which must have been composed at about the same time, his *Risāla al-durriyya,* clearly identifies Khatkīn as the chief *dā'ī.* Khatkīn had asked al-Kirmānī to undertake the responsibility of writing this treatise and its date is in part suggested by Khatkīn's title '*al-ṣādiq al-ma'mūn*' which was bestowed on him by the imam after his appointment as director of the *da'wa.* If Khatkīn had summoned al-Kirmānī from Iraq, the *Mabāsim,* just quoted, which is dated 405 or 406/1015, may reflect the first steps of these two *dāʿīs* to rebuild the *daʿwa* and reinvigorate its operations under a new commission from the imam. *Al-Durriyya* and the treatises by al-Kirmānī that follow it thus come next in this same initiative. The theme of the *Mabāsim* and the rest of the works al-Kirmānī wrote over the next two or three years are certainly all part and parcel of this programme. They were designed to calm the agitation he had observed; but they were also to restore a firmly respectable and valid teaching concerning the imamate and other doctrines of Ismailism.

It is hard now to gauge accurately what the parameters of the troubles in 405 might have been. Al-Kirmānī mentions extremists, meaning those who exaggerated religious doctrine; but he also notes that some others either had renounced their faith or were on the verge of doing so. One outward cause can be traced to the public actions and policies of al-Ḥākim himself, as al-Kirmānī admits. Al-Kirmānī was, accordingly, concerned above all to reject any and all judgements by others of the acts of the imam. No one, he argues, should presume to judge or to question what an imam does or decrees. There is, he says, no abstract standard of rationality in this matter – in fact there exists no external standard at all. Ordinary humans simply should not judge the acts of the imam, any more than those of God Himself.

Al-Kirmānī's pronouncements on this issue are quite frank in confessing to specific policies and incidents that had occurred, which clearly bothered and confused some of al-Ḥākim's followers while providing ammunition for his detractors. One example was his appointment of his cousin to succeed him instead of his son. Another was his practice of riding a donkey in public rather than a horse, or frequently riding by night. But in both cases al-Kirmānī is equally stern in warning against trying to understand or comprehend them. The era of this imam, he notes, is not a relatively quiet and safe period, as was that of his grandfather al-Muʿizz and great-grandfather al-Manṣūr. Extraordinary happenings belong to extraordinary times. Al-Kirmānī betrays at this point his own anticipation of momentous things to come; the imamate of al-

Ḥākim, he feels, will succeed finally in destroying its enemies and achieve its true position as sole ruler of all Islam. Never mind that his wish was not realized; al-Kirmānī in his first year in Cairo thought that it certainly might be. The future of al-Ḥākim was, for al-Kirmānī, even yet more glorious than his past.

Nevertheless, al-Kirmānī took great pains to affirm that there would be another imam to succeed al-Ḥākim, and after him yet another and another. Each specific imam governs a particular period: al-Mahdī, for example, was the fourth of the second series of seven; al-Mu'izz was the seventh of the same series; and al-Ḥākim is the sixteenth imam. There will be, he asserts confidently, an eighteenth, a twenty-first, a twenty-fifth, a twenty-eighth, a thirty-second, a thirty-fifth, and even a fifty-ninth and more to come. Al-Kirmānī's attitude thus involves, on this issue, an insistence that no single imam may be judged or held accountable for what transpires in his era, in part because each is one link in an ongoing chain of imams. It is the whole institution of the imamate that matters ultimately and not necessarily any single imam. Yet he was equally concerned to recognize and to defend the special circumstances surrounding the pronouncements and policies of the imam of his own time, al-Ḥākim. Al-Kirmānī's arguments are at once general and yet also quite specific. He speaks for the imamate as an institution that is critical for Islam historically but at the same time for himself personally. It is noteworthy that all his writings are dedicated to al-Ḥākim.

Another theme that appears throughout his works – one that must have been prominent during these years in Cairo – is concern for the observance of what he calls the double worship (*al-'ibādatayn*[21]). More will be said later about the details of this concept which is central to al-Kirmānī's thought; but here it must be noted how his preoccupation may have played a special role in Egypt. Double worship or observance is simply a regular combination of both works and faith. Its importance in the Ismaili context arises not from what the authorities taught or advocated, but from what their opponents charged them with. Since the Ismailis maintained that true religion must recognize the inner spiritual meaning of all its outward manifestations, some observers accused them of accepting only the esoteric aspects of law and scripture and ignoring the rest. These critics said it was the doctrine of the Ismailis that, once one knew the inner truth, the outer forms ceased to be necessary. Once a person apprehends the spiritual reality behind religious observances, the obligation to perform works no longer applies. Religion becomes a matter solely of inner realities, a concept subsumed under the Arabic term *bāṭin* and for which the Ismailis were often derided as the Bāṭiniyya, the advocates of esoteric meanings.

Despite constant denial of this charge by all the Fatimid authorities, it was a handy axe to threaten them with and it was used by their enemies throughout the period.[22] What makes al-Kirmānī's attention to it important, however, is the probability that some of those whom he labels extremists in Egypt may have, in fact, begun to advocate a form of this teaching. It would be difficult to be more precise. Still, various early Shīʿī groups, known under the general rubric of Ghulāt (exaggerators), had in the past drifted into a doctrine which claimed that ʿAlī and his interpretation (*ta'wīl*) of religion were inherently superior to the revelation of the Prophet Muḥammad. Accordingly, the imams in whom the living interpretation resides are the sole fountain of authentic understanding for all matters of faith. Al-Kirmānī would have found nothing wrong with this latter concept but, against anyone who tried to declare that the 'interpretation' nullifies the revelation or cancels observance of the obligations in law, he objected with all the force of his being. Both the outward and the inner manifestation of religion remain valid and must be scrupulously observed. One without the other is simply false; the *daʿwa* must promote both in equal measure.

Yet more dangerous was a radical development of this same teaching in which some members of the *daʿwa* began to suggest that the imam himself was divine. By this they meant specifically al-Ḥākim alone and not any other imam. The *dāʿīs* responsible for this tendency were fairly obscure figures although the names of three – al-Darazī, al-Akhram and Ḥamza – are known and they were all active in Egypt during the last years of al-Ḥākim's reign. Perhaps al-Kirmānī alludes in the passage above to this type of extremism. But that too is uncertain, for he does not mention the names of the deviants in that treatise. A couple of years later, however, he addressed a special work to al-Akhram who appears then to have been a renegade *dāʿī* whose associates had declared the imam divine, a claim al-Kirmānī says al-Ḥākim denied. This is his *al-Risāla al-wāʿiẓa* which he wrote in Fustat in Jumādā II of the year 408 (November 1017). That year also happens to be the first year of Ḥamza's open preaching of a similar doctrine, as attested in the records of the Druze community. Al-Kirmānī does not mention Ḥamza or al-Darazī, but the context of his remarks must apply to a group that may have included both at one time. What remains unclear is whether his worries in his earlier *Mabāsim* concern this same group exactly and exclusively, or whether their movement developed later. Possibly it took on its more radical form – or the public declaration of it – only in 408 about the time of the later treatise.[23]

The advent of the most serious form of this doctrine, as is also obvious from al-Kirmānī's rebuttal to the questions posed by al-Akhram, may initially have involved a kind of populist approach to the status of the imam. As will be more apparent in analysing the theoretical work of al-Kirmānī, his notion of prophecy and imamate was at its heart highly abstract and intellectual. Likewise, many of his predecessors in the *daʿwa* were profoundly philosophical and their explanation of religion required an advanced knowledge of the theoretical sciences. *Dāʿīs* of the type represented by al-Akhram wanted something else; they longed for direct access to the imam and a down-to-earth understanding of religious doctrine. Rather than being told about the universal intellect and universal soul of a Neoplatonic cosmology, they required real and palpable objects for worship and devotion. The abstractions of al-Kirmānī were probably of little use to them. Certainly many modern readers of his works also despair of being able to grasp what he may have meant or what he thought. The clash between the two sides long ago in Egypt surely pitted irreconcilable forces against each other.

Inexplicably Ḥamza, who was the only one of the three *dāʿīs* to survive the violent reaction to this movement by the populace and the army, ceased his open activities during 409/1018. Al-Darazī and al-Akhram had both by then been killed. Khatkīn continued to direct the official *daʿwa* and quite possibly al-Kirmānī also remained a part of it. Ḥamza and his associates persisted nonetheless. When the trouble first broke into the open, Khatkīn and al-Kirmānī must have wished they could suppress it quickly and easily, but the imam's decrees over the previous decade were quite explicit against engaging in controversy. No one, apparently including the highest authorities of the *daʿwa*, was to delve into another person's religious doctrine. No one should attempt to investigate or conduct an inquiry into what others advocated. Only an imam could do that and he had ordered the community to respect and not to interfere with any one else's form of religious observance except upon specific instructions or commandments directly from him. Despite this general policy, agitation could and did occur, riots and temporary revolts of the soldiers could and did happen. But the official establishment had no choice but to obey, although most assuredly a war of words took place and the hostility intensified.

In 410/1019, Ḥamza recommenced his version of the *daʿwa* only to be driven underground and out of Egypt soon after. The following year was the last of al-Ḥākim's imamate. By then al-Kirmānī had returned to Iraq. The final version of his great masterpiece, the *Rāḥat al-ʿaql,* was assembled in Iraq in 411/1020. When therefore, amidst these difficulties, did he leave Egypt and why? There is no way at the moment to find answers to these questions. His involvement in the local *daʿwa* and its business on behalf of Khatkīn seems to have been of major significance. Khatkīn evidently remained chief *dāʿī* through to the end of the reign; he is certainly listed as one of the five 'opponents' (*aḍdād*) that Druze lore remembers from these final years, the others were the *'ālim al-'ulamā'* Ja'far, the *walī 'ahd al-muslimīn* 'Abd al-Raḥīm, the *walī 'ahd al-mu'minīn* al-'Abbās b. Shu'ayb, and the chief *qāḍī* Ibn Abi'l-'Awwām. Al-Kirmānī is not one of this group, nor is he cited in Druze literature, as he might well have been given his role in Cairo. One explanation is that he never held a prominent post, but a better one is that he had left Egypt by 410 when the final and most important events in this struggle took place.

When then did al-Kirmānī himself die? He was in Iraq in 411 and still active at the time al-Ḥākim disappeared and his imamate ended, and yet there are no writings of al-Kirmānī dedicated to his successor al-Ẓāhir. Accordingly, it is normal to assume that he died in 411 or close to it. Against this at least one work, the *Waḍī'a fī ma'ālim al-dīn,* contains a peculiar passage in which there occurs the typical citation of al-Ḥākim in such a fashion as to mean that it was written during his reign. Immediately thereafter, however, the list of imams continues with al-Ẓāhir and al-Mustanṣir suggesting that, if the author is responsible for these names, he had to be alive until at least 427/1036.[24] As the firmly dated period of al-Kirmānī's life spans only the twelve years from 399/1008 to 411/1020 and no more, one must assume a further extension of it. Still, since each of the surviving works cites al-Ḥākim as the imam of his time, and since the 411 revision of his *Rāḥat al-'aql* seems to come at the end, it is not very plausible that he continued to write after that date. Perhaps he contented himself with an occasional revision of an older book or treatise. If so he might have added a mention of a later imam where useful or required. It is more likely, however, that an early copyist simply inserted these names out of a pious motive to complete a citation the author might have added had he lived. In any case al-Kirmānī himself disappears from our view in the same year as his imam al-Ḥākim.

2
The Works of al-Kirmānī

Given that all we know of al-Kirmānī comes from comments in his own writings, his books and treatises are in effect his biography. For this reason, a hundred years ago it would have been impossible to say much about his life or writing. Even by 1950, the situation was only slightly better, although several of his works had by then emerged from heavily restricted Ṭayyibī collections where they had been preserved unknown to outsiders for almost a millennium. Since then our understanding of what al-Kirmānī wrote, when and for what purpose, has seen a rapid acceleration. Nevertheless, questions remain and it is extremely important that we solve as many of them as possible. They are, after all, the basis on which we locate him and his place in history. But what, for example, is the likely sequence of his works. Why did he write what he wrote and when? Al-Kirmānī was not simply an independent scholar indulging his personal inclinations for knowledge but rather a committed servant of an important cause. His writings therefore served a particular purpose, partly his own and partly that of the *da'wa* he supported. Only when we develop answers to these questions can we begin to see him as more than the author of this or that individual piece of writing.

Inventories Ancient and Modern

Fortunately, direct participation in the internal programme of the Ismaili *da'wa* in Egypt accorded al-Kirmānī a valuable opportunity to amend and to teach his own books and treatises.

It is likely to have contributed to their preservation and popularity among subsequent generations of *dāʿīs*. By contrast, his return to Iraq threatened not only to expose him to the censure of his enemies but to bury his writings in obscurity. Unlike the works of al-Qāḍī al-Nuʿmān, for example, some of which were known to the Twelver Shīʿī *qāḍī* al-Jarājikī,[1] a contemporary of al-Kirmānī, or even the substantially earlier treatises of several *dāʿīs* that were available to the Zaydī al-Bustī, who also lived at the time of al-Kirmānī, there is no obvious record of him or his writings outside of the Ismaili *daʿwa* until much later.[2] But it is hard to determine precisely why some works of al-Kirmānī survived and not others, or why no outsider mentions them.

An even more puzzling fact about them is that many of those still with us contain cross-references and citations to other works of his in such a way that they refer reciprocally to each other. On the one hand, we are fortunate to have the testimony by the author to another of his own titles because it provides sure proof that he wrote the work he mentions. We are thereby spared the problem of authenticity. Yet, on the other hand, because these cross-references occur between two works so that one mentions the other and vice-versa, these citations do not reliably indicate which work came first and which later. Perhaps, since the occasion of his teaching in Cairo allowed him to revise some of his earlier books, in so doing he could add, when appropriate, a note about other places and other titles in his own writings where the same subject had been treated, quite possibly in more detail. Nevertheless one positive result of having this data is that we can be fairly certain of what he wrote, even in those instances where the work itself no longer survives. (A complete list of internal citations to these other titles in al-Kirmānī's own works appears here as Appendix B.)

In this regard, however, it needs to be admitted that despite his crucial position in the *daʿwa* of his time and his undeniable eminence as a writer and thinker, al-Kirmānī's approach met with only moderate success among the generations that immediately followed him. In part, his inclination to philosophical positions which were in opposition to those of his predecessors kept him out of favour. Many, if not most of the Ismaili *dāʿīs*, both before and after him, leaned toward the ideas expressed in the writings of Abū Yaʿqūb al-Sijistānī, who preceded al-Kirmānī by at least one full generation if not two. Al-Sijistānī's brand of Neoplatonic theory, especially with respect to cosmology, became increasingly popular and was certainly accepted by the central *daʿwa*, with the imam's approval, from the reign of al-Muʿizz onward. It shows up clearly in the works of Nāṣir Khusraw and in those of al-Mu'ayyad fi'l-Dīn al-Shīrāzī, both from the time of al-Mustanṣir in the middle of the 5th/11th century. As will become more obvious later in this and the succeeding chapters, al-Kirmānī proposed the adoption of a slightly different system, one derived less from Neoplatonic sources and more from the then current interpretation of Aristotle. Against the others, he therefore urged a carefully thought out but fairly profound revision of the older formulations by earlier Ismaili thinkers in these areas. His teaching was more in line with the great Muslim philosophers, al-Fārābī and Ibn Sīnā – although not a direct copy of their ideas – and he attempted to adjust the articulation of Ismaili thought in their direction accordingly. It should be noted that this tendency did not affect doctrines about the imamate but only those primarily devoted to metaphysics and the cosmic order.

Still, without immediate acceptance, al-Kirmānī remained important, though somewhat neglected, until a Yemeni Ṭayyibī revival of interest in him and his ideas beginning in the 6th/12th century. Once this renewed attention began, it continued and grew and it was thus al-Kirmānī's turn to assume the dominant intellectual position though, in this case, only for this particular *daʿwa*. The Ṭayyibī authorities collected all the older Arabic works they could find and they tended to study and quote from a wide variety of them without regard for the fine points of earlier disagreements. Apparently all the older figures found favour with them. But al-Kirmānī was, for them, arguably the preeminent writer on matters of philosophical, especially of cosmological, doctrines. This development in and of itself is important mainly for the history of Ṭayyibī thought and is not relevant here – it has not received critical study in any event – but such deep concern for al-Kirmānī's works among the *dāʿīs* in the Yemen may have been critical in preserving them. Our only copies all derive, as with most of the other early Ismaili Arabic texts, from the efforts of these same *dāʿīs*. Their devotion to al-Kirmānī proved especially valuable in this regard.

In this particular instance, we are fortunate that a major medieval historian, the previously mentioned Idrīs ʿImād al-Dīn, who was himself the nineteenth chief *dāʿī* of the Ṭayyibīs from 832/1428 until his death in 872/1468, provided a list of al-Kirmānī's writings, with, most significantly, a note about which of them had managed to reach the Yemen. Given what we know about the survival of Ismaili texts, this information is vital in assessing what might now exist. In all likelihood, if the Yemeni Ṭayyibī *daʿwa* did not or could not obtain a copy by the time of Idrīs, no copy remains. The other possible avenues of survival, such as the Syrian Ismaili community, have thus far proved disappointing as a source for the oldest Arabic works.

The printed text of volume six of Idrīs's *ʿUyūn al-akhbār* (pp. 284–8) where he gives a list of al-Kirmānī's works is unfortunately, at least partially, corrupt and it is at the moment unclear whether the errors, some of which are more obvious than others, are due to printing mistakes or to a failure on the part of the scribal tradition. Therefore the list, as given there, requires the emendations which follow here. Idrīs says that he knows of twenty-nine titles that belong to al-Kirmānī. This is an important piece of information and it tallies precisely with what we can discern as well. Unfortunately, our sources for the data about the writings of al-Kirmānī are, in the main, exactly the same as those of Idrīs, namely the citations by al-Kirmānī of his own works. Nevertheless, it is significant that we appear to have exactly what Idrīs had.

Idrīs commences by quoting the opening passage from al-Kirmānī's *al-Risāla al-durriyya* about the appointment by the imam of Khatkīn al-Ḍayf to take charge of the *daʿwa*. He then says that '... of his compositions and writings those that we have found or have come down to us are ....' The list starts with *Rāḥat al-'aql*, which he then describes, followed by the *Kitāb al-riyāḍ*. Next he gives the titles of the various treatises commonly grouped together under the heading *Thalāthat 'ashar rasā'il*, of which only eleven are by al-Kirmānī.[3] The printed text, however, inexplicably omits two of the eleven – *Risālat al-nuẓum* and *al-Risāla al-muḍī'a*[4] – which almost certainly must be added. The titles in this collection are too well known to be in doubt and therefore Idrīs would have included them all. Subsequently, the list cites al-Kirmānī's *al-Waḍī'a fī ma'ālim al-dīn, Tanbīh al-hādī wa'l-mustahdī*, the second part (*al-juz' al-thānī*, 'what exists of this work') of *Ma'āṣim al-hudā wa'l-iṣāba fī tafḍīl 'Alī 'alā al-ṣaḥāba, al-Maṣābīḥ fī'l-imāma* and *al-Aqwāl al-dhahabiyya.*

Two other titles appear in the same list, *Kitāb al-'aqā'id wa lubāb al-fawā'id* and *al-Khazā'in fī funūn al-'ilm wa'l-ta'wīl*, neither of which is attested anywhere else as a work of al-Kirmānī. They are therefore either a corruption in the text of Idrīs or, possibly, errors that he himself made by attributing works of other authors to al-Kirmānī. Both cases will require further research to learn the source of the mistake but, even now, there is almost no likelihood that either is authentically a work of al-Kirmānī.[5]

Significantly, Idrīs next adds a list of al-Kirmānī's works that were not found in the Yemen in his time: 'Of his books that are not to be found in the Yemen and of which he himself mentioned that they are his works, there are ... ' The list is as follows: *Risālat al-fihrist, Risālat al-mafāwiz wa'l-ḥadā'iq, Tāj al-'uqūl, Kitāb maydān al-'uqūl, Fī'l-ma'ād, Kitāb al-naqd wa'l-ilzām, Iklīl al-nafs wa tajuhā, Kitāb al-muqāyis, al-Majālis al-Baghdādiyya wa'l-Baṣriyya* and *al-Risāla al-ta'wīliyya.* To these he also adds the lost first half of the *Ma'āṣim al-hudā.* Here, in regard to these titles, we clearly have the same information that he possessed since all of them have been taken from al-Kirmānī's own citations in the surviving works and which, it would appear, we have. Only one is missing and one lacks a part of its title. Al-Kirmānī mentions a work of his called *al-Waḥīda fī'l-ma'ād*, or simply *Fi'l-ma'ād,* in seventeen separate instances in six different works. Surely it is the same as that listed by Idrīs above as *Fi'l-ma'ād.*[6] It is also doubtful that such a work survived although the title appears in various catalogues of Ismaili manuscripts. Most probably works with that or a similar title are not by al-Kirmānī but rather by a later author. The one title completely missing is a *Risāla* he called *al-Shi'rī fi'l-khawāṣṣ,* which he cited only once and that in his *Mabāsim al-bishārāt.*

Comparing the results of this survey, using both the evidence available in surviving works and Idrīs's list and his comments, it is obvious that the eighteen titles of the books and treatises we have now are most likely the same as those found long ago in the Yemen in the mid-9th/15th century. They are surely all that now exists and we can be fairly certain, therefore, that the corpus of al-Kirmānī's works in our hands is virtually as complete as it is ever likely to be. The lost items number, depending on how Idrīs meant to count, eleven when the first portion of the *Ma'āṣim al-hudā* is included as a separate title. That would make the total twenty-nine as he himself states. By counting the *al-Shi'rī fi'l-khawāṣṣ* but not the *Ma'āṣim al-hudā* more than once, there are still only twenty-nine works in all.[7]

The Chronological Order

A few of al-Kirmānī's works are dated by explicit references but most are not. When dates can be determined, they provide helpful data in determining the turning points of his life – usually the only such information about him which now exists. That evidence was reviewed in Chapter One. It is striking, nevertheless, how little there is and also how the whole of al-Kirmānī's writings focus on the single imamate of al-Ḥākim and thus, in fact, seem to fall between 399/1008, the date of his *al-Risāla al-ḥāwiya,* and the final revision of the *Rāḥat al-'aql* in 411/1020, even though we must presume that his productive years extend back prior to 399. One more treatise carries a fixed date, *al-Risāla al-wā'iẓa,* which was composed in Egypt in 408/1017.

Normally, the internal citations within one author's works provide an indication of the order in which they were written. A mention of another title usually means that it had to have been completed before the one in which it is cited. Occasionally, however, as with al-Kirmānī, the ongoing revision of various works allowed the author to insert citations and cross-references, making firm conclusions about chronological order next to impossible. There is, nonetheless, some useful data to consider. His treatise called *al-Risāla al-lāzima* deals with the commencement of the month of fasting and speaks specifically of events connected to this problem for the year 400/1010. It must, therefore, have been written afterwards, but not long afterwards. The *Maṣābīḥ,* which was addressed to Fakhr al-Mulk, has to be located between about 402 and 407, that is between the appointment – more exactly his arrival in Baghdad at the very end of 401 – and the death of this vizier. The *Ma'āṣim al-hudā* refers to an edict (*sijill*) of al-Ḥākim issued in 401 and thus it must come later than that. *Al-Risāla al-durriyya* comes after Khatkīn's assumption of leadership in the *da'wa* and after he was granted the title *al-ṣādiq al-ma'mūn,* which is likely to have occurred in the year 406. Surely the *Mabāsim al-bishārāt* preceded it, though still from about the same period. The *Risālat al-nuẓum* itself says that it follows *al-Durriyya* as apparently do *al-Raḍiyya* and *al-Muḍī'a,* probably in a series.

Slowly and somewhat imprecisely, this kind of information builds a picture of the probable order of al-Kirmānī's treatises. They seem to belong to two periods defined and separated by his earlier activities in Iraq and the east and a later one in Cairo. By this reckoning his *Maṣābīḥ* might terminate the older set just as he departed for Cairo. Works finished in Iraq would then include the previously mentioned *al-Ḥāwiya* and *al-Lāzima* but also, much more importantly, the polemical *Ma'āṣim al-hudā* which probably belongs to the time of the *Maṣābīḥ,* or perhaps just after it. Both come after his *al-Aqwāl al-dhahabiyya* which the *Ma'āṣim* cites seven times.[8] Here these internal references surely indicate priority since the *Aqwāl* is mentioned in none of al-Kirmānī's other works. The *Aqwāl al-dhahabiyya,* moreover, states carefully that it was written after *Iklīl al-nafs*, the *Muqāyis* and *al-Waḥīda fi'l-ma'ād*, all of which therefore go back to the earliest period in Iraq, as do *Tāj al-'uqūl*, *al-Mafāwiz wa'l-ḥadā'iq* and *al-Naqd wa'l-ilzām*, all three of which are also cited in the *Aqwāl al-dhahabiyya*. Significantly, these last six works, all from the earliest period, are now lost. The only book it mentions that still exists is the *Rāḥat al-'aql*, which must therefore prove that it came both before and after the *Aqwāl* in two different versions.

Of the lesser treatises he wrote in Egypt, the internal citations provide some evidence of their plausible order. First is the *Mabāsim al-bishārāt* and then the *Durriyya*. Next comes *al-Rawḍa* followed by *al-Muḍī'a* and the *Waḍī'a*. Both the *Nuẓum* and the *Raḍiyya* came after the *Muḍī'a*. The *Kāfiya*, which is cited by the *Mabāsim*, would appear to be a product of an earlier phase and quite probably should be pushed back to the Iraqi group. The main problem with dating it so early is that it refers to the *Tanbīh al-hādī*, but this particular citation is reciprocal and is likely to reflect an interpolation, perhaps even added by a copyist.[9] The *Rawḍa* and the *Zāhira* cite each other, as do the *Waḍī'a* and the *Muḍī'a*. In these latter cases, it makes sense that both pairs were under composition at almost the same time, which allowed al-Kirmānī to insert easily the cross-references here.

Three major works reflect what we know of al-Kirmānī's main concerns after coming to Cairo and they, therefore, appear to date from that period. They are his *al-Waḍī'a fī ma'ālim al-dīn* in which he writes at length about the necessity of the double observance of works and knowledge; his *Tanbīh al-hādī wa'l-mustahdī*, which in part refutes a great number of sectarian groups and tendencies; and finally his *al-Riyāḍ*, in which he takes upon himself the task of bringing harmony and proper order to an acrimonious dispute within the *da'wa* proper. It seems that such themes were less appropriate to his role abroad where, particularly for the purposes of the *Waḍī'a fī ma'ālim al-dīn* and the *Riyāḍ*, which are both introspective and oriented toward problems within the *da'wa*, he may have felt that he could or should not speak about such matters in front of a hostile audience. To be sure, based solely on their content, none of these three must have been written in Egypt or between 406 and 411, but the pattern of citations to them and in them supports this conclusion. They are themselves, for example, not cited in the works such as *al-Aqwāl al-dhahabiyya*, which clearly belong to the earlier period but only in works of the later Egyptian phase of his life. The *Tanbīh al-hādī* mentions the *Wā'iẓa* which is dated specifically to 408. The *Riyāḍ* cites the *Waḍī'a*, the *Muḍī'a* and the *Rawḍa*, whereas it is referred to itself only in the *Rāḥat al-'aql*.

Three more works that appear to be authentic but are known only from the citation of their titles – *al-Shi'rī fi'l-khawāṣṣ*, *al-Fihrist* and *al-Risāla al-ta'wīliyya* – cannot be dated. However, it is likely that the *Fihrist* is quite late, perhaps even an effort by al-Kirmānī at the end of his life to catalogue his works for posterity. The *Ta'wīliyya* might represent a generic title and thus refer to various treatises that have as their purpose some sort of interpretation of Qur'ānic verses (*ta'wīl*) rather than a specific work with that title. It might also have been a collection of such pieces.

The one difficult exception to all these rules is al-Kirmānī's most important and largest book, the *Rāḥat al-'aql*, which cites as many as fifteen of his own titles and in turn is mentioned in eight, five of which involve reciprocal citations, i.e. they refer to it and it refers to them. The *Riyāḍ* is an interesting example. It is cited nowhere else but in the *Rāḥat al-'aql* where it is mentioned three times. However, it refers itself to the *Rāḥat al-'aql* fifteen times. The best solution to this quandary is that first proposed by J. van Ess, namely to recognize an earlier and a later recension of the *Rāḥat al-'aql*.[10] Accordingly, there must have existed a version composed by the author in Iraq which he subsequently brought with him to Egypt. It is that version which is cited in a number of other works including the *Aqwāl al-dhahabiyya* and the *Maṣābīḥ* as well as later writings, such as the *Waḍī'a*, the *Riyāḍ* and *al-Durriyya*. When, after returning to Iraq, he finished the ultimate draft of the *Rāḥat al-'aql*, he simply embellished the text with additional citations to his own earlier works, perhaps even inserting longer passages about them such as appear now in its introductory chapters.

Form, Subject and Content

Up to this in the book we have examined carefully the information in and about al-Kirmānī's writings with a view to explaining both what he wrote and what any of this material might indicate about his life. There is much more, however, particularly in the actual content of the various works which reveals, perhaps step by step, if the chronology just established is valid, what issues concerned him at various points in his career in the *da'wa*. To an extent, there is no reason to assume that his focus changed radically; the problems that had occupied him earlier certainly continued to be important. We also know that he held on to some works, most notably the *Rāḥat al-'aql*, and added to them over the space of possibly the whole decade from 400 to 411. Still, interesting bits of evidence suggest a development in his efforts and a transformation from an earlier Iraqi to later Egyptian perspective, from that of an outsider looking toward the centre to an insider struggling to shore up and fortify the core in the face of serious internal dissension in the *da'wa* and the threat of decay and disintegration.

Two small treatises *al-Ḥāwiya* and *al-Lāzima*, the first of which is dated firmly to 399, provide the earliest evidence we have about al-Kirmānī's activities. The *Ḥāwiya* has as its full title 'The Comprehensive Treatise on Day and Night.' It was composed by the author in response to a query from a member of the *da'wa* about which of the two came first and which second. This issue is related to the priority and position of speaking-prophets (*nāṭiq*, pl. *nuṭaqā'*) vis-à-vis founders (*asās*).[11] Quite brief – only ten pages in Ghālib's edition[12] – it cannot in any sense be considered 'comprehensive' or of much significance for the larger understanding of al-Kirmānī. What it reveals, however, is that by 399 al-Kirmānī was high enough in the *da'wa* for him to be consulted on matters like this, and that as the epistolary form of the treatise demonstrates, his *responsa* were sought and obviously valued by his subordinates and colleagues. The *Lāzima*, which is 'The Binding Treatise on the Fast of the Month of Ramaḍān and Its Commencement',[13] is another reply to an inquiry, in this case, about the problem of when to begin the month of fasting. The Ismailis used a calculation based on scientific astronomy whereas the Sunnis insisted on an actual visual sighting of the new moon. On occasion the two methods could result in an early commencement of Ramaḍān (and thus also an early beginning of the feast at its conclusion) relative to the rest of the population. A notable instance of a serious difference – two days – occurred in the year 400 and caused a good deal of friction over the issue. The treatise indicates that orders emanating from the imam that year required the commencement of Ramaḍān two days prior to the eventual sighting of the new moon. Obviously, that could have, and probably did, place a special burden on those Ismailis outside Fatimid domains. Al-Kirmānī, however, defends the rule. But again, the crucial point is to observe that writing this work is a part of how he performed his role as a ranking authority in the *da'wa*.

The next group of treatises by al-Kirmānī, the *Iklīl al-nafs wa tājuhā* ('The Garland of the Soul and Its Crown'), *al-Mafāwiz wa'l-ḥadā'iq* ('Deserts and Gardens'),[14] *al-Muqāyis* ('The Comparing' or the 'The Measurements'),[15] *Tāj al-'uqūl* ('Crown of the Intellects'), *al-Waḥīda fi'l-ma'ād* ('The Matchless Treatise on the Hereafter'), and *al-Naqd wa'l-ilzām* ('Criticism and Consequence') are all lost. Likewise we have no trace of his *al-Majālis al-Baghdādiyya wa'l-Baṣriyya* ('The Baghdādī and Baṣran Lectures') which must also belong to the period of his career prior to his arrival in Cairo. The first six are, as noted earlier, mentioned in the *Aqwāl al-dhahabiyya* and they were certainly written prior to it. From the brief notice given there it would seem that all of them concern, at least in part, problems of the soul. The *Muqāyis* was a refutation of the Ghulāt and their ilk, most likely in regard to claims of metempsychosis or transmigration of the soul (*tanāsukh*). In the same vein another undatable treatise, the *Maydān al-ʿaql*[16] ('The Arena of the Intellect'), is cited in the *Rāḥat al-ʿaql*[17] as having the same purpose, namely to counter those who uphold a doctrine which insists that the reward for goodness accrues in this world by means of the return or rebirth of souls in a higher or lower form here rather than in a hereafter – a concept al-Kirmānī rejects utterly.

The general subject of the *Naqd wa'l-ilzām* cannot be surmised merely from its title nor from the one reference to it found in the *Aqwāl al-dhahabiyya* (p. 95), but what al-Kirmānī does say about it in the latter is interesting. In a section where he specifies that the animating force that directs the body does not arise from the body but rather comes to it from outside and is its life, which is otherwise called its soul (*nafs*), he identifies 'living' or 'alive' (*ḥayy*) in respect to the body with its 'life' (*ḥayāt*), i.e. its soul. The soul is life and is alive. What is alive or living has life; when life departs, body and soul separate, although the soul continues to live. Here he points out that the famous *qāḍī* ʿAbd al-Jabbār b. Aḥmad denied that life (*al-ḥayāt*) is a thing that lives (*al-ḥayy*). He continues, 'We have examined what he said carefully and explained his error in this matter in our book known as *al-Naqd wa'l-ilzām*.' This ʿAbd al-Jabbār, who once taught in Baghdad until becoming the *qāḍī* of Rayy, was the leading Muʿtazilī theologian of his time. He died in 415/1024 and was thus a contemporary of al-Kirmānī. He was also quite hostile to the Ismailis and it would be important to know more about their attitude to him specifically and his writings. Unfortunately, this single reference is all there is.

To judge solely from the pattern of internal citations, the next treatise by al-Kirmānī could well be his *al-Maṣābīḥ* which itself cites only the *Rāḥat al-ʿaql* but is mentioned by both the *Aqwāl al-dhahabiyya* and the *Maʿāṣim al-hudā*, two other works we place in the Iraqi period. We have discussed this treatise, which was addressed to the Buyid vizier and which contained a broad reaffirmation of the requirement of the imamate and of that of al-Ḥākim specifically, at some length in Chapter One. Based solely on this evidence, therefore, the *Maṣābīḥ* would have to be slightly earlier than the *Aqwāl* which in turn precedes the *Ma'āṣim.* Accordingly, it is unlikely to have come just before his departure but rather somewhat earlier, though still after 402/1011.

One of the major offenders on the subject of metempsychosis was the famous physician and philosopher Abū Bakr al-Rāzī, who was, for the Ismaili writers from his own time onward, the paradigmatic arch-heretic. Ismaili attacks on this al-Rāzī go back to the encounter between him and the *dā'ī* Abū Ḥātim al-Rāzī which the latter recorded in his *Kitāb a'lām al-nubuwwa.*[18] Nearly a century later al-Kirmānī composed his own refutation of Abū Bakr's *al-Ṭibb al-rūḥānī*[19] which he called *al-Aqwāl al-dhahabiyya* ('The Golden Sayings') and is now available in a critical edition by Ṣalāḥ al-Ṣāwī. Although al-Kirmānī recognized and admitted the pre-eminence of Abū Bakr in the medicine of physical ailments and their treatment, he strongly contested al-Rāzī's qualification to administer to the illnesses of the soul. In the former field he is a vigorous stallion who gallops at will, but in the latter he is a dried up and withered limb devoid of benefit. In the opinion of al-Kirmānī, the maladies of the soul – its deficiencies and defects – can only be cured by the medicine of prophetic religion as dispensed by the living imam and his *da'wa.*

In his introduction to the *Aqwāl,* al-Kirmānī provides a valuable note about the works he had already written, namely the *Iklīl al-nafs,* which he says covered governance (*siyāsa*), the relative merits of various species of animals and the human in relation to other kinds of created beings, and what the soul goes to after death. The latter subject was also covered, he says there, in his *al-Muqāyis* and in the *Risāla al-waḥīda.* Only after he composed these works did he come upon a copy of Abū Bakr's *al-Ṭibb al-rūḥānī* and was moved to write a rebuttal of it.[20]

After this attack on Abū Bakr al-Rāzī, al-Kirmānī took on the great 3rd/9th century literateur and theologian al-Jāḥiẓ, whose *Kitāb al-'Uthmāniyya* was anathema to all Shī'īs for its abject failure to recognize the superiority of 'Alī b. Abī Ṭālib over 'Uthmān, or for that matter, over either Abū Bakr or

'Umar. It was, moreover, obviously pro-Abbasid. Our copies of the *Maʿāṣim al-hudā wa'l-iṣāba fī tafḍīl ʿAlī ʿalā al-ṣaḥāba* ('The Protecting Links to Guidance and the Validation of the Superiority of 'Alī Over the Companions'), al-Kirmānī's answer to this work of al-Jāḥiẓ, are missing the first portion. The surviving text commences with the thirty-first section (*faṣl*) of the third chapter (*bāb*) on the virtues and excellences that belong exclusively to 'Alī among the Companions. That third chapter has sixty-four sections. Next come sixteen sections in chapter four on the virtues that both Abū Bakr and 'Alī have in common followed by only four in chapter five on Abū Bakr's own merits. That all this is keyed to the work of al-Jāḥiẓ is shown by frequent references to the *ṣāḥib al-ʿUthmāniyya* or even to al-Jāḥiẓ himself.[21] Significantly, Abū Bakr is not there denied all respect, in part because in the year 401 the Imam al-Ḥākim had decreed that, in contrast to a long-standing perception of the Shīʿa in general and to specific actions ordered by al-Ḥākim earlier in his reign, the Companions were to be mentioned henceforth only for the good they had once done. This benevolent attitude was to be particularly extended to Abū Bakr for what he had done in the time of the Prophet and of which the Prophet approved. That is why, says al-Kirmānī, in this book, 'we recall here the virtues of Abū Bakr.'[22]

Yet one more item from the Iraqi phase of his career is another refutation of a non-Ismaili, this time the Zaydī imam al-Mu'ayyad bi'llāh Aḥmad b. al-Ḥusayn, who reigned in the Caspian region and died in 411/1020. This man's denunciation of al-Ḥākim's right to the imamate was rejected by al-Kirmānī in a treatise he called *al-Kāfiya* ('The Effective Treatise in Refutation of al-Hārūnī al-Ḥusaynī the Zaydī').[23] Since the *Kāfiya* is cited in the *Mabāsim al-bishārāt*, it would have been composed prior to al-Kirmānī's arrival in Egypt.

Having reached Cairo, al-Kirmānī observed there, to his great disappointment, general chaos and malaise. We quoted at length in Chapter One the sad introduction he wrote to his first work in Egypt, the *Mabāsim al-bishārāt* ('The Smiles of Glad Tidings').[24] This treatise he dictated to the *mu'adhdhin* of al-

Azhar, one ʿAlī b. al-Ḥusayn b. Aḥmad al-Iṣfahānī. Obviously, al-Kirmānī felt compelled to undertake a programme of restoration and rescue and he commenced with this treatise which is a strong and quite practical defence of the imamate of al-Ḥākim, a subject about which he had by then written at length in previous works. The *Mabāsim* is, moreover, strikingly specific in its details, both about the unusual circumstances of al-Ḥākim and his times and the activities of the *daʿwa* under him. He mentions two cases where the imam had dispatched edicts to individual *dāʿīs* in the east whom he names. And he identifies Maḥmūd of Ghazna and the Abbasid caliph al-Qādir as the major enemies of the Ismailis and at the end, with upbeat confidence, he predicts their defeat and overthrow by the 400th anniversary of the Prophet's leaving this world, i.e. the year 411.

Next al-Kirmānī wrote the treatise he called *al-Risāla al-durriyya fī maʿnā al-tawḥīd wa'l-muwaḥḥid wa'l-muwaḥḥad* ('The Glittering Treatise on the Meaning of God's Absolute Oneness, the Unifier and the Unified').[25] This work, like the *Mabāsim*, takes note of the unhappy state of the *daʿwa* not long before and how, under the circumstances then prevalent, many thought they would perish. At that point, he says,

> the aid of God came to them in the reflection of His friend, the son of His Prophet [i.e. al-Ḥākim] ... who lit for them what had been dark and illuminated for them what had been obscure. He did that by selecting from among them the one most truthful in speech, the most trustworthy in execution, most correct in religion, the one having the firmest stand of obedience, the longest to serve. That is Khatkīn al-Ḍayf ... and he appointed that man the gateway [*bāb*] to his mercy with the title *al-ṣādiq al-ma'mūn*, the *dāʿī al-duʿāt*.

Almost certainly, then, al-Kirmānī had been commissioned by Khatkīn to write this treatise as an answer to a question posed in a meeting of the *dāʿīs*. What is not exactly clear in the preceding passage alone is whether, at this juncture, he had in mind a series of additional works based more or less on the same initiative. In the collection of his *Rasā'il*, as commonly found today under the title *Thalātha 'ashar rasā'il*, the order runs from *al-Durriyya*, through the *Risālat al-nuẓum fī muqābalat al-'awālim* ('A Treatise on Correlations in the Conformity of the Worlds'),[26] *al-Risāla al-raḍiyya* ('The Agreeable Treatise'),[27] *al-Risāla al-muḍī'a* ('The Penetrating Treatise'),[28] and then *al-Lāzima*, *al-Rawḍa* ('The Garden'), *al-Zāhira* ('The Luminous Treatise'), *al-Ḥāwiya*, *Mabāsim al-bishārāt*, *al-Risāla al-Wā'iẓa* ('The Admonishing Treatise'), and *al-Kāfiya*. However, that is not the order in which they were composed. *Al-Ḥāwiya*, *al-Lāzima* and *al-Kāfiya* are early, as previously noted. In terms of al-Kirmānī's immediate objectives in dealing with problems encountered in Egypt, his *al-Rawḍa* came after the *Durriyya*, followed by *al-Muḍī'a* and then *al-Nuẓum*. The *Zāhira* is associated with the *Rawḍa*, the full scale *al-Waḍī'a* with the much shorter *al-Muḍī'a*, and the *Raḍiyya* with the *Nuẓum*. His *al-Wā'iẓa*, which was written in the middle of 408, is not clearly related to any particular one of these although we must assume that these other works came at the same time as it.

In a few cases within this series, al-Kirmānī himself admits that he wrote a particular item because someone had brought to his attention a problem or misunderstanding prompted by one of the earlier *risālas*. Thus, for example, *al-Nuẓum* has the purpose of clarifying issues that had been discussed in *al-Durriyya*. Three of them in part or whole concern the writings of Abū Ya'qūb al-Sijistānī. One, the *Zāhira*, is a response to a member of the *da'wa* who had asked if a certain treatise, ascribed to al-Sijistānī, is actually his. Al-Kirmānī concludes that it is not. In the *Rawḍa* he criticizes al-Sijistānī for the latter's views about the meaning and significance of the terms *al-azal* (the Eternal), *al-azalī* (eternity), and *al-azaliyya* (eternality), and he summarizes Chapter (*iqlīd*) Twenty-one of al-Sijistānī's *Kitāb al-maqālīd*. The author of the *Rawḍa* does not agree with his predecessor. In a similar way, in his *al-Muḍī'a*, he objected to a doctrine explained in the Twenty-eighth *iqlīd* of the same work by al-Sijistānī. There al-Kirmānī, however, carefully apologizes for pointing out the errors he found in it. He did not intend, he says, to censure the older author especially given his elevated rank and noble status within the *da'wa*.

While engaged in writing various of these works, al-Kirmānī accepted a larger challenge. A member of the *da'wa* had written to him asking his help in providing an introduction to the study of Ismaili doctrine. 'Oh, brother,' replies al-Kirmānī, 'your letter has arrived in which you mention that you have not found among the books of the masters, may God sanctify their spirits, something which would constitute a primer for the novice at a level prior to the reading of the major tomes, nor what at the same time would indicate clearly the rules by which God is to be worshipped.' To remedy the situation he wrote a special work which he called *al-Risāla al-waḍī'a fī ma'ālim al-dīn* ('The Pure Treatise Concerning the Hallmarks of Religion'). Near the same time he wrote his *al-Muḍī'a*. The two words *waḍī'a* and *muḍī'a* appear to derive from the same Arabic root, both meaning 'bright' or 'shining'. Yet the term *waḍī'a* in the title of the larger and more substantial work may convey more of a sense of 'clean' and 'pure' as understood from its associated connotation of ritual purity and ablution (*wuḍū'*). Does al-Kirmānī imply that this work sets out the pure, Ismaili teaching on the fundamental points it covers? Its theme, to be sure, is the double observance (*al-'ibādatayn*) which lies at the very heart of the author's teaching. As such we will return to examine the details in a later chapter. Here it is important to place it in the context of his activities in Egypt. Al-Kirmānī was pursuing an agenda which involved the reassertion, as forcefully as possible, of the need for both faith and works – that is, knowledge and practice, *bāṭin* and *ẓāhir*, an understanding of the intellectual requirements in faith along with the performance of ritual acts and the observance of the religious law. In those times of trouble, he devoted this one treatise to a carefully reformulated manual of what must be taken as Fatimid and Ismaili official doctrine. We can assume that it was needed because some members of the *da'wa* had either lapsed or questioned the need to perform their outward religious duties and that the enemies of the Ismaili movement made much of this fact.

To be sure, a charge of having abandoned the law in favour of some form of inner or esoteric interpretation was commonly levied against the Philosophers and the Sufis as well as Ismailis, but in this instance the threat was internal and beginning to grow at the very heart of the imam's empire.

The worst of the unorthodox in Egypt were al-Akhram and his associates. Against them and their disregard for religious law and its regulations, al-Kirmānī directed his *al-Risāla al-wāʿiẓa.* Like his other defences of the imamate of al-Ḥākim, this one is specific and contains important information about the claims evidently put forth by al-Akhram at that time or slightly before. This group, among other doctrines, apparently regarded al-Ḥākim as the final imam because, they claimed, he is himself eternal. There were several examples of earlier Shīʿī groups that had fallen into the error of insisting that a certain imam had not died – a position known by the technical term *wāqifiyya,* meaning to stop the continuity of the imamate as a whole and deny that it has been passed on to a successor. Having decided that al-Ḥākim was himself eternal, however, it was relatively easy for them to begin also to claim that he is an incarnation of God Himself. This latter step is, of course, much more unorthodox and generally constitutes blasphemy.[29] To counter this trend or the threat of it, al-Kirmānī insists adamantly that the imam – any imam – is human and occupies a temporary portion of time. There will be many, many more imams to come, he says. The rebellion of al-Akhram was obviously serious; it was highly offensive to the regular Ismaili *dāʿī*s and the *daʿwa.* But al-Kirmānī notes that we have been enjoined by the imam not to further stir up religious trouble. The arguments of the pen had, in this case, to suffice, at least in respect to the involvement of al-Kirmānī.[30]

The work called *Tanbīh al-hādī wa'l-mustahdī* ('The Exhortation to the Guiders and the Guided'), composed after the *Wāʿiẓa,* fulfils a similar niche to the *Waḍīʿa* but not at quite so basic a level. Al-Kirmānī wrote it, he says, because he had observed that the Muslims (*ahl al-qibla*) had broken up into factions in accord with their individual views. They had abandoned true religion. This is a common enough theme but it defines the special purpose of this work. A portion of it covers the standard doctrines of the Ismaili *da'wa* on the imamate, the *sharī'a*, faith, purity, prayer, alms-giving, fasting, pilgrimage, *jihād*, obedience to the imam, the oath and covenant, knowledge of the interpretation (*ta'wīl*) and others, each in their own chapter. A central portion, however, serves as an occasion for refutations of the Philosophers (*al-mutafalsafūn*), the Mu'tazila and the 'proponents of inference and speculation' (*ahl al-istidlāl wa'l-naẓar*), the Ash'ariyya, 'the proponents of juridical analogy' (*ahl al-qiyās*), 'the proponents of personal opinion and effort' (*ahl al-ra'y wa'l-ijtihād*), 'the proponents of considering what is best' (*ahl al-istiḥsān*), 'the proponents of imitation' (*ahl al-taqlīd*), those who uphold consensus (*ahl al-ijmā'*), those called the Twelver Imāmiyya, the Zaydiyya, and the Ghulāt, here specifically the Nuṣayriyya and the Isḥāqiyya.

The final work of his Cairo efforts, if it in fact belongs to that phase, is the book *al-Riyāḍ* ('The Meadow'). Only the revised version of the *Rāḥat al-'aql* came later. The full title of the *Riyāḍ* varies from citation to citation but it is usually indicative of exactly what the work contains and what its purpose was. It runs as follows: *Kitāb al-riyāḍ fi'l-ḥukm bayn al-shaykhayn Abī Ya'qūb al-Sijistānī wa Abī Ḥātim al-Rāzī – qaddasa Allāhu arwāḥahumā – fī Kitāb al-iṣlāḥ wa Kitāb al-nuṣra wa iṣlāh mā jarā baynahumā fī dhalika wa iṣlāḥ mā ahmala iṣlāḥahā min Kitāb al-maḥṣūl*, which may be translated as 'The Book of the Meadow in Judging between the Two Masters, Abū Ya'qūb al-Sijistānī and Abū Ḥātim al-Rāzī – may God sanctify their spirits – in Regard to the Book of Correction and the Book of Support, and in Correcting What Occurred between Them in that Regard, and in Correcting What He Neglected to Correct from the Book of Results.' That is, of course, a cumbersome and exceedingly awkward title. It does, however, say that the book concerns three extremely important Ismaili *dā'īs* who preceded al-Kirmānī and whose writings needed, in his view, rectification. It is obvious, moreover, that a fairly serious dispute about doctrine is involved. In fact al-Kirmānī's *al-Riyāḍ* constitutes a rare chance to look inside the *daʿwa* and observe the thinking of several generations of *dāʿīs* ranging from Abū Ḥātim and Muḥammad al-Nasafī, the author of the *Maḥṣūl*, at the beginning of the 4th/10th century, to that of al-Sijistānī in the middle of it, and ending with al-Kirmānī at the start of the next.

Despite its importance, however, the *Riyāḍ* is not a pleasure to read; it is highly obtuse and complex.[31] The issues in dispute are hardly obvious; they concern the soul, first intellect, prime matter, whether human souls are a part or a trace of the universal soul, in what manner the human being is the fruit of this world, the relationship of motion and rest to prime matter and form, the divisions of the world, the meanings of *al-qaḍā'* and *al-qadar*, whether or not Adam brought a religious law, and finally various problems in defining the absolute oneness of God. It might have been dismissed or left to highly trained experts for whom it was clearly written, but it enjoyed unusual favour in the later Ṭayyibī *daʿwa*.[32] Al-Kirmānī himself, moreover, accorded it a remarkable endorsement in the final version of his *Rāḥat al-ʿaql*, a work which one might think greatly surpassed the *Riyāḍ*. But in a discussion of what books should precede the *Rāḥat al-ʿaql*, al-Kirmānī says: 'Let the reader keep the *Riyāḍ* before his eyes since it is within the horizon of this one and there is explained in it what will assist him and strengthen his ability to discern the truth in the matters about which they disagreed. He should not be satisfied with reading it once only but rather ten, twenty or even fifty times until what it contains becomes a fixture of his soul.'[33] Considering that the *Riyāḍ* dealt with an internal dispute among fellow *dāʿīs*, that is an especially powerful recommendation. It is likely, therefore, that al-Kirmānī wrote it with an agenda in mind which is not readily apparent to us, but it is also characteristic of this phase of his writing that he saw fit to correct other members of the *daʿwa*.

In the next chapter we will look more carefully at al-Kirmānī's attitude to his predecessors in the *daʿwa*, a subject he approached with great tact and delicacy, but nevertheless with a deliberate purpose and programme. He wanted to change the teachings and move them more toward what he believed was the current scientific viewpoint, but he did not intend to rebuke his fellow *dāʿīs* or cast doubt on their sincerity. That is why, in part, when it came to acknowledging these same forefathers in the preface to his *magnum opus*, the *Rāḥat al-ʿaql*, he did so with fulsome praise. Only obliquely does he suggest, however strongly, that a properly prepared reader must have previously read his *al-Riyāḍ*. That book is the antidote; it makes the necessary adjustment to the older writings about scientific matters. The *Rāḥat al-ʿaql* simply presumes that the reasons behind the new concepts of al-Kirmānī, i.e. the basis of his alterations, are clear enough and that the older doctrines no longer stand. He feels, moreover, free not to argue with such earlier *dāʿīs* as al-Nasafī or al-Sijistānī again. The grand summation of his thought builds a great and positive edifice, a city of God on earth and in heaven, rather than pick out and quarrel about the weaknesses and defects of the *daʿwa* in the past.

Thus the final work of al-Kirmānī contains only the best, a distillation of all knowledge, collected into a city, the city of knowledge, the city for which the Prophet himself had said that ʿAlī, and thus the imam, is its key and gateway. This extremely important image of knowledge and the concept of the city is the subject of our last chapter as it was in the career of al-Kirmānī. We cannot now know what process of development brought him to this achievement, but a survey of his works has begun to reveal, admittedly with some speculation, what steps it consisted of, and approximately when and under what conditions they occurred. With one or two exceptions, when the internal references in and to the *Rāḥat al-ʿaql* are ignored, the rest of al-Kirmānī's writings seem to have a sequence and to divide roughly into an earlier phase in Iraq and a later one in Egypt, although the material in them is not precisely differentiated. Still, his refutations of non-Ismaili thinkers such as Abū Bakr al-Rāzī, the *qāḍī* ʿAbd al-Jabbār, al-Jāḥiẓ, the Zaydī imam of his time, and others, belong to the period of his residence in the east, whereas the major exhortations to his own colleagues on behalf of al-Ḥākim and his imamate, and his

3

Al-Kirmānī and the *Da'wa*

At the end of his account of various instructions that had been given by previous imams to selected followers of theirs, al-Kirmānī inserted the following passage which can only apply to himself. The text represents, therefore, the imam's personal commission to him and contains, in all likelihood, a portion of the mandate given him prior to undertaking his duties as *dā'ī*. It must represent a special charge by al-Ḥākim to al-Kirmānī just prior to his taking up or, perhaps more probably, resuming his post in Iraq. The context is thus quite interesting and the implied subject is certainly indicative of a theme that al-Kirmānī himself repeated over and over in his writings, especially from the later years of this imam, when this issue apparently assumed critical importance. What al-Kirmānī repeated of it runs as follows:

> Al-Ḥākim bi-Amr Allāh, may God keep him, in his instructions to Aḥmad b. 'Abdallāh, when he dispatched him to the province of Iraq, declared:
>
> 'Observe our commandment in regard to the worship of God, the exalted; seek our approval by acting in accord with the orders of God, the highest; and give new life to the Sunna of our forefather, the apostle of God, God bless him and keep him, through the summons to the absolute oneness of God. You will find no increase in that toward God or toward us other than in closeness. But warn the opposition that resisting our command will give no increase in respect to God except in greater distance from Him. Maintain the prescribed acts of

obedience, such as instituting regular prayer, observing righteous deeds, executing fully all trusts. These imbue you with the resulting goodness and cause you to inherit a place of nearness to God. Turn all the faithful in the direction of adherence to the bonds of religion and fulfil the terms of the covenant and of fealty which is obligatory on them and which is recorded in the books of their deeds. Inform them that our intercession is valid for none who are not among those who act in accord with the Book of God, the exalted, and the Sunna of His apostle, God bless him and keep him, and by means of our command worship God by obeying us. Proclaim this to the friends of God and of us as our own words.'[1]

This highly unusual passage occurs in the *Tanbīh al-hādī wa'l-mustahdī* in the fourth chapter entitled 'On the Gist of the Instructions [*waṣāyā*] of the Imams to their Followers [*ashyā'ihim*] in Regard to the Acts in the Laws'. Clearly then its purpose is closely connected with the doctrine of double observance; note, in particular, how the law is to be scrupulously obeyed and the ritual acts, such as prayer, carefully observed.

That, however, is only one lesson to draw from it – one which will occupy our attention in the next chapter. Another is to note that it supplies us with direct evidence of how the imam personally guided his *da'wa*. Obviously he was in touch with the leading *dā'īs*, even those abroad in distant and hostile territories. This fact was not previously in doubt but there exists little, sometimes no, evidence for it or about it in the surviving literature. Al-Kirmānī's writings, however, are noteworthy for the information they supply and the confirmation they offer of the Ismaili *da'wa* in action.

Already it is clear that al-Kirmānī was frequently asked for his opinion on various issues, or requested to write a work of one kind or another to aid the programme of the *da'wa*. It is also evident from his statements that authorization for his effort came from above, from the imam himself. He mentions a number of edicts and letters of instruction, perhaps like the one above that was issued to him personally. These emanated from Cairo; some were specific answers to requests from individual *dā'īs*[2] and others were of wider application, addressing the leaders (*shuyūkh*) of the *da'wa*.[3] Al-Kirmānī states explicitly that no one is to teach anything having to do with religious doctrine without an authorization from the imam.[4] And in several places and contexts, he quotes from al-Ḥākim or from al-Ḥākim quoting his predecessors.[5]

Numerous references to the *ahl al-da'wa* or *ahl al-da'wa al-hādī* ('Adherents of the *Da'wa*' or 'Adherents of the Rightly Guiding *Da'wa*') and the mention of geographical places as varied as Jīruft in the province of Kirmān, where al-Kirmānī's subordinate worked, but also to Ṭabaristān, Jīlān, Shīrāz and other locations both east and west begin to reveal the breadth and scope of this operation. Al-Kirmānī says, in fact, in his *Maṣābīḥ* that 'the *da'wa* on behalf of al-Ḥākim bi-Amr Allāh, the Commander of the Faithful, on whom be peace, exists everywhere and there is no country without it nor any section of the territory of Islam that does not have a *dā'ī* in it to appeal for obedience to God through His imam and to declare the absolute oneness of God through him, either outwardly when possible or inwardly when not.'[6] 'Obedience to the highest authorities, who are the imams, is not valid except by following those below them who have been put in office to provide guidance, either close up or from a distance, by instituting obedience to them outwardly and inwardly. Accordingly, the believer must submit to the imam [through them].'[7]

The *da'wa* is thus a hierarchy of subordinate authorities appointed to teach and guide (*al-ḥudūd al-manṣūba bi'l-ta'līm*).[8] All believers – that is Ismailis, the adherents of the imam – attend sessions of instruction and learn there from higher authorities the elements of religion and its science and wisdom.[9] Thus, a major duty of the *dā'īs* is to provide various kinds of education for the followers of the imam. This may cover only matters of practice and the outward acts of worship, which is a job, al-Kirmānī says, assigned to the *ma'dhūn*, one of the lower ranks in the *da'wa*. Above, the full *dā'ī* takes over and begins to teach the intellectual component of religious observance.[10] Even at this level there are differences in the abilities of the *dā'īs*: some are knowledgeable but do not have a gift for speaking and teaching. They need the instruction provided by the *ḥujja.*[11]

Such important details of how the *da'wa* functioned, as found now scattered throughout his writings, help explain what al-Kirmānī himself was doing. It must be admitted, nevertheless, that although the *da'wa* was surely his main concern, he seldom tells us as much as we would like to know about it. Since he wrote his books for members of the *da'wa,* he did not normally need to explain its activities to them. But there is one exception to this observation. Possibly, as there always had been, deviant or dissident *dā'īs* did exist, and some who once were obedient and later turned away. Equally there can be no doubt that al-Kirmānī was deeply bothered by such events. In the admonishing treatise he wrote to al-Akhram, the *Wā'iẓa,* he responds to a question this man was asking about doctrinal principles in such a way as to show that al-Akhram had probably been a *dā'ī* who was now a dissident. The exchange, however, is interesting on several levels.

Al-Akhram had questioned what purpose there could be in speaking about the 'innovation' (*al-ibdā'*) which transcends spiritual and physical being – referring to the doctrine of creation which is of considerable importance in Ismaili thought. Al-Kirmānī does not really answer him directly in this treatise but he does remark there, 'the knowledge of that ... is with us, the body of *dā'īs* [*ma'shar al-du'āt*], as a trust coming from the masters of it, the apostles of God, deposited with us in order for us to convey it to those who rightly deserve it among those who have affirmed their supremacy.' Al-Akhram has broken that trust but, says al-Kirmānī, 'should you return to the way of observance in accord with its true conditions, that knowledge will be extended to you as well.'[12]

From our modern vantage point, we may note here that al-Kirmānī would have been hard pressed to answer al-Akhram's question with full honesty since it presupposes a doctrine of his predecessors, al-Nasafī and al-Sijistānī, that he himself did not really accept. If al-Akhram and his followers were rebels and thus in danger of excommunication, these two well regarded *dāʿīs*, most especially al-Sijistānī, had been full members of the *daʿwa* and their works were highly prized, perhaps even above those of al-Kirmānī. But it was the function of the *daʿwa* to deal with opponents of all kinds. The rebels from their own ranks were but one category. The main opposition were countless non-Ismaili groups of varying persuasions, nearly all hostile. With enemies enough, why therefore fight with friends? The answer is both complicated and interesting. We will return to it later.

Here it is important to observe the *daʿwa* in the person of its most eloquent spokesman taking on its detractors both from within and from without, whether rebellious former *dāʿīs* or members of anti-Ismaili groups of many kinds. The devils, says al-Kirmānī, are everywhere and they even pretend to be scholars and among the people of truth (*ahl al-ḥaqq*), but they write books simply to delude the people.[13] Yet he also warns frequently that he himself cannot be completely forthright in what he says for fear of his work falling into the wrong hands and the clutches of those not worthy of it.[14] The position of a *dāʿī* cannot have been easy. Away from Cairo, there was a constant threat of denunciation by the opponents of the Ismailis. But at the same time it was al-Kirmānī's duty to pursue the opposition wherever it might be. The *dāʿīs* should, under certain conditions and restrictions, investigate carefully all matters of science that do not accord with their faith.[15] His opponents had achieved a high level of scholarship and, because the doctrines he and his *daʿwa* advocated were equal or better, although similar in many ways and were certainly just as intellectually sophisticated, the truly serious threat lay with the most erudite of them.

For al-Kirmānī and the Ismailis of his time, these were the Philosophers and the Muʿtazila, both of whom taught doctrines that less knowledgeable enemies accused them also of having adopted. Even now the Ismaili *daʿwa* of that era is known for its philosophy and for the philosophical elements in its doctrine as it was then propagated. Less understood, but nevertheless important, was how Mu'tazilī ideas and concepts influenced the way Ismaili thought came to be expressed. Mu'tazilism was a fairly early school of theology in Islam and, as such, it often set the main agenda for discussion. Accordingly, later Islamic theologians could not avoid the issues that the Mu'tazilīs had first defined and declared essential. Moreover, by the time of al-Kirmānī, major sections of the Shī'a had adopted a Mu'tazilī position in regard to these same topics. But the Ismaili *da'wa* had actually accepted neither philosophy nor Mu'tazilī theology and its *dā'īs* were at pains to make the difference between their teachings and those of these two groups perfectly clear. This was, however, not always an easy task.

Reading al-Kirmānī's writings, especially his major work the *Rāḥat al-'aql*, which is full of philosophical concepts (as are many of his other works), quickly proves that he knew philosophy as well as almost anyone at his time. He had certainly studied Aristotle carefully. It is likely that he was completely familiar with a range of sources either real or attributed from ancient Greek, although there is no evidence that he knew Greek. Likewise he must have read the works of the leading Muslim philosophers, particularly al-Fārābī with whom he shared a number of metaphysical and cosmological principles. But there were specific differences as well.

Against the Philosophers al-Kirmānī directed a chapter of his *Tanbīh al-hādī wa'l-mustahdī*, and it is there where we see the clearest expression of what he found wrong with their approach. Sections of his *Rāḥat al-'aql* likewise reveal his disagreement with them. One difference is that, according to al-Kirmānī, the Philosophers (and the Ghulāt) believe only in the intellectual component of worship and observance and they refuse to admit the requirement of works and ritual acts.[16] They also maintain a doctrine that insists that the human soul begins life with a predisposition toward goodness; it can on its own both discover what is right and wrong and move itself, by itself, toward salvation. In their view, those who grasp the truth in the sciences cease to have need for the laws. All this is simply not correct according to al-Kirmānī. The soul has no adequate predisposition but rather urgently requires outside instruction and a programme of habituation that instills in it virtues it cannot obtain on its own. In one passage he states that these are wisdom, purity and probity (*ḥikma, 'iffa* and *'adāla*), which are given only by the acts prescribed by the law, not by philosophy.

The Philosophers think that what their intellect has determined is, in fact, the true reality of things. In adjudging the rules by which the physical world functions, i.e. in the arena of sensation, they may be correct, al-Kirmānī admits, but they err in trying to imagine the realm of the intelligible. For example, they hold that what has its existence from the first cause, which they believe to be intellect, is also an intellect. If the first cause is God and all subsequent beings are of the same genus – that is, intellect – necessarily all existing things are God.[17] In their view creation at this level occurs as emanation (*fayḍ*), but, notes al-Kirmānī, an emanation has the same genus as its source. Thus God and the intellects would be of the same genus which is impossible.[18] These are merely examples of his critique of the Philosophers whom he obviously understands quite well and yet separates himself from. Concepts in philosophy may, of course, be valid but the Philosophers have no special authority for them and on certain points they have been misled into errors that are simply unacceptable. By rejecting the guidance of the *da'wa* they have resorted to conjecture and opinion that, however intellectually astute, is nevertheless false.

The Mu'tazila, for al-Kirmānī, include the Zaydīs who have, he says, adopted Mu'tazilī doctrine.[19] They share to a degree the same basic fault as the Philosophers. They believe, he notes, that the human intellect can determine basic religious truths on its own. For them the mind is a source of knowledge and, even without the Prophet, we would know, for example, of the absolute oneness of God. It need not be taught, according to them, since the intellect will perceive it by itself. This point of doctrine can be proven intellectually and thus a teacher is not absolutely essential for it. The implication in al-Kirmānī's refutation is that if some elements of religious knowledge do not require the prophets, then the need for them diminishes. The

Philosophers were generally accused of believing that philosophy is superior to religion because it provides access to the true intellectual meaning behind the law without requiring either the authority of a teacher or the law itself. All this is wrong, says al-Kirmānī. Even Muḥammad could not determine the law without divine guidance. The Prophet did not rely solely on his intellect in adducing the rules of religion, how then could the Mu'tazila?[20]

With the other Islamic sects the issues of difference are less subtle and they involve little ambiguity that might cause confusion. Their errors could never be attributed to the Ismailis as, by contrast, those of the Philosophers and the Mu'tazila were on occasion. The Ash'arites, he comments, believe in attributing bodily characteristics to God. They hold that He is knowledgeable because of possessing a knowledge that is itself eternal.[21] The Twelver Shī'a, some of whom were also Mu'tazilīs, opposed the Ismailis principally on the question of the imamate, according to the statements of al-Kirmānī. The Twelvers, he says, believe that the imam is superior to the Prophet and refuse even to admit that 'Alī was above the other imams. They hold, moreover, that the imams perform miracles and that these are signs of their office. Al-Kirmānī counters that the imams are known by an explicit designation (*naṣṣ*) and thus do not require miracles to confirm this fact. But, he adds, this is not to deny that the other imams, who have unique access to the support of God and His blessing, have miracles, since that which was revealed to Muḥammad and returned to the heavens thereafter is preserved solely in them. Nevertheless, if the knowledge possessed by an imam is itself miraculous, the performance of miracles is not an essential component of the imamate.[22]

Al-Kirmānī's Sources

In many respects the scholarly resources available to al-Kirmānī reflect his interests and they are more or less clearly delineated in his works and in the comments just discussed. Certainly he had read carefully the writings of a vast array of ancient and contemporary authors. A number of citations in his books and treatises, however, help make what we know about him more specific. One quite striking aspect is his references to textual passages from pre-Islamic scriptures which he quotes in either Hebrew for the Torah or Syriac for the Gospels. So unusual and noteworthy are these instances of a Muslim writer using the Biblical text, that they drew the attention of the modern scholarly world to al-Kirmānī even before any of his works had been published in Arabic or studied in any other way.[23] On each occasion of these quotations he wrote the passage in Arabic script but in the original language, not in translation. Does this fact mean that he knew these languages or did he have someone else transcribe them for him? That they appear in at least four of his works,[24] however, suggests that he himself knew what he was writing. But how had he learned either language and why? Was he born a Jew and later converted as did a number of other major figures who served the Ismaili imams, such as Ya'qūb b. Killis, the vizier under the caliph-imam al-'Azīz and the author of an important book on Ismaili law, or a later vizier Abū Naṣr Ṣadaqa b. 'Alī al-Falāḥī, a Jew who likewise converted?[25] In contrast, however, to these cases, where the Jewish origin of the individual is well attested, nothing of the kind was ever claimed for al-Kirmānī.

Other than Biblical sources, al-Kirmānī refers to but does not quote such material as the *Book of Amthāl* (Proverbs),[26] the *Sīra* (biography of the Prophet), masterpieces of language and belles-lettres, such as the *Kitāb al-'ayn* by Khalīl b. Aḥmad and the *Jamhara* of Ibn Durayd,[27] the Qur'ānic commentaries of Ibn 'Abbās and al-Kalbī,[28] the works of *maghāzī, āthār* and *akhbār,*[29] and treatises of various opponents of which he disapproved, including, in addition to those already cited, a work by Abū Ḥanīfa on legal stratagems (*Kitāb al-ḥiyal*)[30] and Abū Bakr al-Rāzī's 'Doubts About Galen' (*Shukūk 'alā jālīnūs*),[31] to name two from vastly different fields. There is therefore no reason to question al-Kirmānī's erudition; one may confidently surmise that he had read everything then available and, most remarkably, some in languages other than Arabic.

Nevertheless, it is clear that he regarded his ultimate source to be the imams. In addition to al-Ḥākim, he cites by name al-Mu'izz for a book called *Ta'wīl al-sharī'a* on intellectual and spiritual interpretation.[32] He mentions a list of books by the imams in his *al-Waḍī'a* which is remarkable for including those by imams of the earlier prophets, e.g. the *Iqlīmas* by Simeon the Pure or a work by Peter (*Kitāb Buṭrus*).[33]

Beyond the imams, whom he never ceases to recognize as the ultimate source of knowledge, he credits his colleagues in the *da'wa*. Al-Qāḍī al-Nu'mān, the great jurist and historian who wrote under the imams from al-Qā'im to al-Mu'izz, particularly the last of these, occupies a special place. Al-Kirmānī recommends his *Da'ā'im al-Islām*, the *Īḍāḥ* which he notes comprises 5,000 folios alone, the *Mukhtaṣar al-āthār, al-Iqtiṣār, Sharḥ al-akhbār, Kitāb al-ṭahāra, Kitāb al-maghāzī* and *al-Manāqib wa'l-mathālib.*[34] Most important, in the introduction to his *Rāḥat al-'aql* (pp. 22–3), he provides a list of the works by his fellow *dā'īs* that should be read prior to reading it. Just as the progress of the soul toward its salvation must commence with matters most accessible to it, i.e. those that involve the senses, and only after mastering them can it move on to the purely intellectual realm, so, too, it is essential, says al-Kirmānī, for the reader of his book to study the works which properly come before it. Having read them it will be easier to comprehend this one, the *Rāḥat al-'aql.* First of all comes the Book of God; but next on the plane of outward acts and deeds are the works of al-Qāḍī al-Nu'mān. In matters of spiritual interpretation and other items related to the intellectual observance of religion, he cites the book of the caliph-imam al-Mu'izz, the *Kitāb ta'wīl al-sharī'a,* the books of Ja'far b. Manṣūr al-Yaman, and others by leading masters in the *da'wa,* such as Abū Ḥātim al-Rāzī, Muḥammad b. Aḥmad al-Nakhshabī (al-Nasafī), Abū Ya'qūb al-Sijzī (al-Sijistānī), and others 'may God raise their rank upon their return (to Him).' Since he does not name any of the others, we must assume that these five *dā'īs* stand out in his mind.

Immediately following the list just given, al-Kirmānī turns to his own earlier works and there mentions the *Tanbīh al-hādī* as the place to begin. Next comes the *Waḍī'a fī ma'ālim al-dīn*, the *Maṣābīḥ*, the *Riyāḍ*, several of his *risālas*, as arranged, he says, in the *Fihrist*, but above all the *Riyāḍ* (to be read over and over again). Finally he recommends his *al-Waḥīda fi'l-ma'ād*. Not to follow his instructions in this matter, he goes on, will harm the soul, causing an injustice to it, because 'this book along with those books and the knowledge in them is like the antidote that furnishes one with good health and a wonderful reward, but this book alone without those is like a poison that leads to perdition and the pain of everlasting torment.'

While it would be unreasonable not to take him at his word, between the lines there is here evidence of another attitude toward some of his predecessors. Why emphasize the *Riyāḍ* so extravagantly? We know, in fact, that it contains his critique of a long-standing debate among three of the *dā'īs* whose works he had just recommended. It also includes al-Kirmānī's own corrections of various doctrines originally advocated by al-Nasafī which had not been suitably dealt with, according to him, by either Abū Ḥātim or al-Sijistānī, the two other parties in this dispute. Thus, in it, al-Kirmānī rehearses a century of doctrinal conflict among the *dā'īs*. Al-Nasafī's work the *Maḥṣūl*, from the earliest years of the 4th/10th century, came first and subsequently Abū Ḥātim wrote a well-known correction of it, his *Iṣlāḥ*. Al-Sijistānī found the corrections by Abū Ḥātim to be incorrect and he composed a 'support,' his now lost *Nuṣra*, in defence of the positions taken by al-Nasafī. Finally, al-Kirmānī decided that he should bring harmony to this affair but, in fact, he sought instead to criticize all three and provide his own answers to the same problems. We can see that, of course, despite al-Kirmānī's disclaimer.

The *Riyāḍ* therefore provides a clear picture of the *dā'īs* struggling to arrive at what any one of them would accept as sound doctrine. But, rather than agree, they in fact disagreed and engaged in fairly vociferous debate about the issues that remained unresolved. Al-Kirmānī's attitude is therefore instructive; read the *Riyāḍ*, he advises, to learn there about what is not, in his mind, acceptable in the older teachings of the *da'wa*. Thereafter, but only then will his own contributions become clear and tenable. He thus admits that there are flaws in the older doctrines and they must be corrected. The capital question then is what were they and how did al-Kirmānī propose changing them?

One set of doctrines from the earliest period of Ismaili thought is apparently not involved immediately in this particular debate. That is the cosmology which features notably the angels Jadd, Fatḥ and Khayāl, and the seven heavenly letters which together form the Arabic phrase *kūnī-qadar* (= *k, u, n, i, q, d, r*). Our only detailed account of this doctrine comes from a work written by Abū 'Īsā al-Murshid in the time of the caliph-imam al-Mu'izz, but outside observers recorded it as the teaching of the Ismailis as early as the year 300. Several authors, such as al-Sijistānī, repeat various parts of it as if it were standard doctrine. The whole scheme includes, moreover, other concepts which related to the first created being called *al-sābiq* (the Preceder) and the second *al-tālī* (the Follower). The first of these is often called also the Pen (*al-qalam*) and the second the Tablet (*al-lawḥ*). Later these elements are rearticulated within a Neoplatonic interpretation of the same or a similar system.

Most of this plays almost no role in the cosmology advocated by al-Kirmānī and it does not accord well with his ideas about the order of creation and the hierarchy of intellects, as will become apparent in later chapters of this book. Nevertheless, he does, at least, mention each of these older doctrines in such a way that it would seem that he had accepted them, although perhaps only nominally. Significantly, the *Riyāḍ* is our source for many of them, although they also appear in other treatises.[35] Al-Kirmānī thus leaves a distinct impression that such concepts are residual in Ismaili thought at best and were not necessarily current in his time. Does this attitude reflect the facts or is it merely an expression of al-Kirmānī's own point of view?

In a similar way there were problems with a number of philosophical doctrines in the writings of al-Nasafī and, even more importantly, in those of al-Sijistānī. As one major example, the

Riyāḍ deals at length with the doctrine of the soul or aspects of it. Al-Kirmānī had little patience with the earlier view of the soul, as also with other matters these masters had taught. Though often called a Neoplatonist by modern scholars, he tried to promote doctrines that contradict many notions central to the classical Neoplatonism of its Greek founder Plotinus and what entered Arabic literature under the false title *Theology of Aristotle* but which actually derived from the *Enneads* of Plotinus. For these Neoplatonists, including al-Nasafī and al-Sijistānī, there is a universal soul of which the human soul is a part. The human being participates in the spiritual realm through its soul. In a not dissimilar manner, there is a single universal intellect of a higher rank which is, in fact, all intellect; its realm is one and does not break up into separate parts or separate beings. For al-Kirmānī, as will become readily apparent, intellect is divided into ten separate intellects and none of them is exactly equivalent to the universal intellect or universal soul of his predecessors. Soul, for him, is simply not a universal being but is rather the particular animating form of the individual living body which commences its existence when the individual itself comes into being. This is not yet the place to review these differences in the necessary detail, but it is enough to illustrate in brief how serious were the discrepancies of doctrine between al-Sijistānī and al-Kirmānī.[36] They were both loyal supporters of the Fatimid imams and highly esteemed members of the *da'wa* acting on their behalf, but in certain areas of thought, they were nonetheless widely separated.

For al-Kirmānī the problem was to insert as gently as he could a new teaching into an older system with as little violence to it as possible. He would change it from within by adjusting it in the direction of his newer understanding of these matters. He certainly realized as well that the system he advocated was just then becoming widely accepted by philosophers and other scientists. A major example is the work of his contemporary Ibn Sīnā with whom he shared a good deal. Not the least was the latter's rejection of an older Ismaili teaching about intellect and soul that had been taught to him by his father and brother who were both Ismailis.[37] Still, al-Kirmānī, whatever his differences intellectually, saw his predecessors as colleagues. The work of the *da'wa* would not have been successful without them. They were all participating together in one joint enterprise, and to illustrate this principle forcefully, near the end of his *al-Riyāḍ*, he offers the following image as his explanation of how the *dā'īs* and the *da'wa* share their common experience and knowledge.

> When the author of the *Maḥṣūl*, may God have mercy on him, undertook to exercise his judgement and expend his utmost efforts, he performed the duty of the *da'wa* and those who adhere to it. He opened the gates to its significant traits by the books of his that he wrote for those who stood in hope of it. When Abū Ḥātim, may God have mercy on him, corrected what he corrected of it, many of the people thought that it was on his part a censure of the author of the *Maḥṣūl*, despite the author of the *Iṣlāḥ*'s apology for that in his own book. Thus they found fault with him and were against him for it. But that was an erroneous assessment on their part and a deviation from the truth. The matter was not as they had imagined. The speaking-prophet [*nāṭiq*] realized that, with respect to the arrangement of the subjects that comprise the sciences of religion, they are too numerous to be comprehended by any single individual other than the imam, or for one group only to safeguard them. Accordingly, he designated for this purpose a large number of individuals below the office of the imam who are to collaborate among themselves in the pursuit of all the sciences and in their preservation and safekeeping. Such persons include the twelve *ḥujjas*, each of whom learns from those righteous imams who were appointed by God, the exalted, to assume the reins of guidance, God bless them all, about the most obscure of matters, both the hidden and obvious aspects of them, commensurate with their own abilities and strengths in understanding and comprehension. In this they are to provide guidance for others similar to the way the imams, on whom be peace, confer enlightenment and knowledge. Religion is in them like a single individual who is composed of its parts and they are to him like the senses by means of which things are perceived. If some item escapes one of them, another will per-

> ceive it without the perception by the second implying any fault in the first that failed to perceive it or in any other of the senses. That being so, the correcting by Abū Ḥātim, may God increase his rank, of what he corrected in the book *al-Maḥṣūl* was not a reproach to it nor a belittling of its author and should not be taken as a condemnation of either of them. Rather, it is as we have just said. The individuals assigned to correct the sciences of religion are like the senses. If one of the senses fails to perceive some item in the realm of the physical world, it will not escape the other which will instead cooperate to assist it in fulfilling the duty of religion and confirming the intention of the Lord of the universe.

Thus, late into his discussion of the strident argument between Abū Ḥātim and al-Sijistānī, al-Kirmānī, who at that point had turned away from the two of them and now undertook his own 'correction' of matters concerning *tawḥīd*, introduced and excused himself as a colleague in the *da'wa* who, rather than condemning his predecessor, al-Nasafī, or belittling his contribution, feels the obligation to participate cooperatively with him and them in a common enterprise. The passage constitutes itself a remarkable view of how the Fatimid Ismaili *da'wa* functioned on a theoretical level, at least ideally; it reveals a good deal about the way in which Ismaili thought came into being and about al-Kirmānī's own view of his personal role in the process.

4

Double Observance by Works and Knowledge

The Problem of the *Bāṭin*

Almost all the Shīʿa accept that the imams are those described in the Qur'ān as *al-Rāsikhūn fi'l-ʿilm* ('Those firmly versed in knowledge').[1] After the Prophet Muḥammad, they and no one else, save God Himself, therefore know with precise accuracy the true meaning of the sacred word. The problem is whether that true meaning is contained in and derived – albeit by the imams alone – from the literal text only. Or does it depend on some less obvious or hidden, inner powers that operate independently and at a level beyond, above or behind the outwardly manifested scriptural symbols? If the revelation is *tanzīl,* is its *ta'wīl,* its interpretation, connected to it by the rules of evidence and logic or not? If so, then all learned masters of the Islamic sciences will have equal access to it. If not, and it is known solely through the teaching of an imam, does such knowledge replace the revelation or merely enhance it? In the latter case the esoteric teaching conveyed by the imam adds to what is available in the plain meaning of the sacred word. It thus goes beyond it into a new dimension. The issue that causes a problem, however, is whether both remain valid. Does the inner sense in any way modify or cancel the exterior, or perhaps, make it superfluous?

Islamic heresiographies identify a surprisingly large number of early Shīʿī groups that subscribed to doctrines upholding the exclusivity of the *ta'wīl* alone and condoning neglect of the *tanzīl*. For most of them an event had occurred: usually the coming of a particular person – a messiah, prophet, imam or his heir – who had disclosed the inner meaning of the holy scripture and therefore provided those privy to this kind of knowledge a means to avoid the outward obligations of ordinary Islamic duties, such as prayer, fasting, pilgrimage and alms-tax. If a believer understands what these *sharīʿa* - imposed rites and rituals really signify, according to this line of thinking, they cease to be incumbent upon that person in their literal form, having been thus transposed into something spiritual which no longer has a referent in the corporeal or physical world. If, to use Arabic terms, the literal wording of the law, its *ẓāhir*, is replaced by its 'true' spiritual meaning, its *bāṭin*, then only the latter applies. In short the ritual prescriptions of Islamic law cease to be required and the person who has acquired access to the *bāṭin* may, accordingly, stop observing them.

It should be stressed that while many of the Ghulāt or Shīʿī extremists were accused of this tendency – as well as the Philosophers, Sufis and others – it also tainted dissident sections of the early Ismāʿīliyya. Among the latter, moreover, from the beginning, there was both a general admission of the importance of the *bāṭin*, or the esoteric, inner meaning of the law, as it exists through the teaching of the imam, and equally, of an expectation of a future time when the *sharīʿa* would cease to hold its normative value because it will have become unnecessary. It will have been nullified by the advent of an era without law upon the coming of the messiah (one writer referred to this as Adam's paradise). At that time there will be only *bāṭin* and no *ẓāhir*. At the root of much of Shīʿī thought, it seems there is a dilemma that was often exploited and made into a dangerous deviation from the ordinary Islamic doctrine about the nature of the messianic era and of the signs of its coming. A number of individual renegade movements among the Ismailis, prior to the time of al-Ḥākim, can be cited for evidence of this, including most especially the Qarmatians, who broke away from the mainstream Fatimid *da'wa,* and for whom there is ample evidence of open disregard for traditional Islamic law and ritual. Early Ismaili preaching concerning the messiahship of Muḥammad b. Ismā'īl, the grandson of the Shī'ī Imam Ja'far al-Ṣādiq, which was a major feature in the public message of the pre-Fatimid *da'wa,* compounded this almost natural tendency. If this figure is already the *mahdī* (the messiah), as some claimed, rather than merely a person expected to reappear as such in the future, then it would also be logical to hold that the era of Muḥammad and Islam has been rendered obsolete, having been replaced by that of his ultimate and final successor.

Yet, even without the historical questions of a specific event or the coming of a particular person, the notion of a *bāṭin,* which is not somehow rationally supposed in its evident wording, is troubling and obviously fraught with difficulties for those who subscribe to this position and who also wish to defend it intellectually. The most pressing question is why should both exist? Why should a believer continue to observe the outward literal patterns of religion when only the inner meaning has any real significance? One answer given by some is that the literal and symbolic form of the truth, as codified in the law, is necessary to promote the welfare of those humans who lack the mental capacity to grasp the true reality which it only expresses in a convenient and accommodating form. The elite few who have great intellectual gifts will not require the imposition of such mere approximations of the truth, but they can know it directly in its most pure state and therefore can, theoretically, dispense with common religion. These are, by common agreement, the Philosophers among whom such antinomian tendencies certainly also existed, as they did for the non-conforming Ismailis. The same might also be said of many Sufis.

All this illustrates the complex danger inherent in insisting on the double aspect of religious observance and its meaning, if one is clear and present and the other hidden and obscure.

The threat that some form of secret knowledge alone might be taken to replace ritual observance was a constant worry to an establishment intent on a policy of public legitimacy and of universal acceptance by all Muslims. The Ismailis could never quite escape this problem. It hung over the movement from the beginning and continued. Their enemies were always ready to accuse them of it, whether actually justified or not. But perhaps at no time was the danger more palpable than during the later years of al-Ḥākim's reign. The combination of heightened enthusiasm for the Cairo caliphate and a corresponding influx into the capital of uncontrolled, dissident preachers imbued with doctrines building in one way or another on the notion of the superiority of the *bāṭin* over the *ẓāhir*, and the corresponding supernatural powers that it gives the imams as keepers of the inner meaning, created unusual opportunities within the Ismaili fold for the extremists. The Ismaili *da'wa* must have seen all this as a mixed blessing, wanting, on the one hand, to benefit from the energy then flowing into its cause, but fearing, on the other, the damage that could result from the already well understood antinomian proclivities of some of these same enthusiasts. The birth of rebellious movements, at least as they appeared in Cairo at that time in the preaching of al-Darazī, al-Akhram and Ḥamza, must have renewed in the *da'wa* old anxieties.

What was the actual role of the *da'wa* in these unusually difficult circumstances? This is an awkward question because, for all the theoretical material about it that exists in one source or another, there is little that says exactly how it functioned in practice and who belonged to it, or even what authority it had in these specific circumstances.[2] Al-Kirmānī's own statements are, under these conditions, of unusual value since he was both an eye-witness and a leading spokesman for the *da'wa*. The incident of the rebellion and the necessity of al-Kirmānī's presence in Egypt shows, moreover, the double edge to the establishment's concern. Most clear in the evidence we have already looked at is al-Kirmānī's role in shoring up the *da'wa* by defending its understanding of doctrine against that of al-

Akhram, and possibly many of the others. Less perceptible is the larger issue: that of the general question of the exact relation of *ẓāhir* to *bāṭin,* and of Islamic observance as a whole to its purely intellectual and rationalistic counterpart. Al-Kirmānī was himself a philosopher and an intellectual; his speciality was theory and the theoretical sciences. But was knowledge (*'ilm*) in any way for him superior to practice (*'amal*) such that the former could suffice for faith in lieu of the latter? That it was al-Kirmānī, the foremost Ismaili scholar of his generation, who was asked to address this issue reveals that the threat to the official *da'wa* was only a part, perhaps merely a symptom, of a larger problem that those in power hoped to resolve with his help. The authorities were interested not just in confronting one immediate instance of these difficulties which had begun to go out of control but of reconfirming a doctrine that would deal with the root issues that had caused it originally and on which it fed.

Insisting on the *Ẓāhir*

The general thrust of this issue had already engaged al-Kirmānī prior to his arrival in Cairo. The whole tenor of his writings supports a clear and consistent policy of rejecting those who would ignore the outward forms of religious observance. In all of his works he refers to his own *madhhab* ('doctrine') as *Ahl al-'ibādatayn* ('those of double observance' or 'the partisans of double veneration' – to use two possible translations). The Arabic term *'ibāda* means 'observance,' 'veneration,' 'adoration,' 'service,' 'pious works,' or 'divine worship'. *'Ibād* (plural of *'abd*) are servants, i.e. God's servants. *'Ibāda* is the service and veneration due God by His servants and subjects. The primary sense in this context is the standard Islamic notion of *'ibāda* as the observance of the prescriptions of the law for rites and rituals, as well as acts and thoughts of obedience to and worship of God. Al-Kirmānī relies on all aspects of this complex term but what distinguishes his doctrine from other writers, including earlier Ismaili authorities, is the dual form of the term itself, i.e., *ʿibādatayn,* which he obviously preferred in order to make it as concrete and unambiguous as he could. The observance of those who combine both knowledge and practice (*ʿilm* and *ʿamal*) is, he says, more noble than that of those who abandon either one or the other.[3] To do so is characteristic, according to him, of both the Ghulāt and the Philosophers.[4] But it is decidedly not true of his own *daʿwa*! The surviving literature of the Ismailis is, in fact, unanimous in this regard. And indeed all the writers who preceded him stress a similar teaching, though none quite as strenuously. It became a hallmark for al-Kirmānī and no other doctrine in his thought stands out quite as much.

It is worth noting, however, that the whole subject of knowledge and practice is not simply subsumed under the terms *ẓāhir* and *bāṭin,* which apply to only one aspect of it. Whereas, in the standard discussion of Ismaili doctrines, the issue of greatest concern often is the relationship between the exoteric and esoteric understandings of scripture and the law, al-Kirmānī, who was a fully competent theologian, saw the larger problem which involves matters of faith and works and whether or not being *muslim* is the same as being *mu'min.* What constitutes faith and what are the required works? And how are the two related? Are all Muslims believers or does belief apply to a narrower category? On these classical issues in Islamic theology, al-Kirmānī and his predecessors stipulated that a believer (*mu'min*) must observe all aspects of both faith and works. One might be considered a Muslim for less but not a believer.

Works (*ʿamal*) involve both the performance of moral duties and prescribed ceremonial acts and thus are only partially described by the notion of practice. Moreover, the distinction between *ẓāhir* and *bāṭin* applies more to how a person understands the meaning of a ritual act, a good or evil deed, or an aspect of scriptural interpretation, but it can also be used in relation to faith which is primarily an internal or mental element of religion, and works, which are open and active manifestations of it. Al-Kirmānī refers to all this by the term *ʿibādatayn,* and it seems likely that he intends to formulate in this manner a comprehensive statement of all these issues.

While this point was of constant concern to him and reappears continually in his various works, one among them not merely expresses it abstractly but actually demonstrates it systematically by outlining a detailed programme for implementation. This is the treatise he called 'The Bright Treatise' or 'The Pure Treatise' (*al-Risāla al-waḍī'a*) 'Concerning the Hallmarks of Religion' (*fī ma'ālim al-dīn*). His use of the term *waḍī'a* from the verb *waḍu'a, yawḍu'u,* to be pure, bright or clean, may convey the connotations of ritual ablution prior to prayer which is, in addition to the idea of 'brilliance', one of its aspects and, although it probably forces the lexical context of the word, this might have been intended as a figurative suggestion of the treatise's purpose.[5] It is a purifying treatise and thus reflects the correct doctrine – a teaching that will bring with it purity.

That al-Kirmānī should pointedly undertake to reaffirm the details of ritual observance and practice by composing such a work is noteworthy. He and others of the philosophical wing of Ismailism advocated *sharī'a* Islam. That much is not in doubt. He, like his major philosophical predecessor al-Sijistānī, repeatedly stresses the importance of the law and works alongside faith – practice with knowledge, *ẓāhir* with *bāṭin.* What is significant, in this instance, is al-Kirmānī's insistence on carefully delineating the content of outward (*ẓāhirī*) compliance as if he is attempting to restate for those who followed him and the official *da'wa* exactly what a fully observed Ismaili theology contains. In line with this goal, the work itself opens with a chapter entitled 'On Proclaiming the Rule for the Worship of God that it be a Double Observance by both Knowledge and Practice.' Al-Kirmānī then proceeds to outline both these scrupulously, commencing with the primary understanding in the two forms of worship, which is knowledge, followed by the second, which is practice. Chapters four through seventeen each contain brief statements of the principal items of creed: *tawḥīd,* angels, prophets, *awṣiyā',* imams, scriptures and *sharī'as* ('laws,' in the plural), existent beings, nature, hierarchies, allegiance to the hierarchy, the interconnection of existent beings, *ta'wīl,* intellect, soul, *hayūlā,* form, *bay'a, 'ahd* and *mīthāq.* Together these sections constitute slightly less than 40 per cent of the whole work. The later parts deal with practical worship and observance (*al-'ibāda al-'amaliyya*) and contains chapters on the following: *shahāda,* prayer (including ablutions and funerals), alms-taxes, fasting, pilgrimage, *jihād* and virtuous behaviour (*al-akhlāq*). This second part occupies approximately 50 per cent and is especially detailed on prayer and pilgrimage.

The part covering practice follows, as might be expected, al-Qāḍī al-Nu'mān's *Da'ā'im al-Islām* wherever appropriate and often might be taken as a synopsis of this classic handbook of Fatimid legal materials. Al-Qāḍī al-Nu'mān was the recognized expert in this area. A preliminary appraisal concerning the relative emphasis of subject matter between the two indicates that al-Kirmānī devoted more space to pilgrimage and less to *jihād* than his predecessor, but these slight differences are probably not significant.

A point of historical interest is that it ends with a chapter on decorum and tutelage (*ādāb* and *wasāya*), using this theme to insist on the proper conduct of believers vis-à-vis their own *dā'ī* or his representative. The message is that one should not attempt to exceed one's assigned place and status. This might be read as a common admonition for loyalty in the ranks but, in light of the current of dissent that al-Kirmānī faced from Ismaili extremists, to emphasize this theme in such a way, especially as a conclusion to the section on practice, is historically significant as well.

Above all, however, the work is dominated by the theme of double observance (*al-'ibāda al-'ilmiyya wa al-'amaliyya*) and the absolute necessity for the believer both to have knowledge and to perform works. True, he admits, works (*'amal*) or the physical duties of the sacred law are its exoterica (*ẓāhir*), and knowledge (*'ilm*) is its esoterica (*bāṭin*). One is the product of prophecy and the other of the Prophet's executor (his *waṣī*). The metaphor al-Kirmānī prefers in this instance is that of two parents. The imam, he says, inherits both prophetic authority, the *nāṭiqiyya*, as well that of the Founder, the *asāsiyya*, in the same manner as a child inherits from two parents.[6]

He proceeds to establish the necessity of both by setting forth a parade of citations from the Qur'ān and *ḥadīth* which speak either about knowledge or works or both. He says, 'The prophet-messenger summons people to God's worship and he issues the rules (*qānūn*) for it as they are connected to two things, each of which is subject to commands and prohibitions – one of these is knowledge (*'ilm*) and the other is works (*'amal*).' Accordingly, for example, the Qur'ānic passage 'Invite to the way of your Lord with wisdom and beautiful preaching' (16:125) requires the interpretation of wisdom in two ways. It is divided into knowledge and action (*'amal*).[7] Whoever worships God by one of the two forms of worship (or observance) without the other is blaspheming in that which is left out. 'Of the two forms of worship, whoever worships God by knowledge alone without manifesting such worship through works, which is the other of them and by means of which the soul acquires that form which makes it eternal, will have no station in the afterlife nor will his knowledge bring him salvation on the Day of Resurrection.'[8] 'In serving God, the exalted, he who appeals to works alone is a one-eyed devil (*dajjāl a'war*) and he who insists on knowledge alone is a satan (*shayṭān*).'[9]

The world itself – that is the physical world – is the abode of actions, of works (the *dār al-'amal*),[10] and the 'observances which involve acts that are a training for the souls are compulsory; the acts are the laws themselves and their regulations and rules.' 'The acts are the laws of the prophets and they are a training for the souls and its means of moving from potential being to permanence and ultimate reality.'[11] One can no more dispense with physical rituals and acts than can a ship's captain neglect the upkeep of his boat if he expects to cross the seas safely. The soul's journey, its progress through the terrestrial world, depends on the vessel it travels in and that vessel is its body. The body must be maintained and rigorously controlled by the soul. But the opposite is not true. The soul serves its own end, as does the body because it is merely the soul's instrument.

The soul should not become subservient to its instrument. In part, that is why it needs these regulations that come to it from outside.

But perhaps the most striking expression of this doctrine of double observance occurs when al-Kirmānī speaks of the believer who has received true guidance and is considered therefore an observant member of the righteous community – a member of the Shī'a about whom Ja'far al-Ṣādiq declared 'You are truly in paradise.' 'But,' says al-Kirmānī, imagine, 'how reprehensible of a person to be one of those in paradise alongside people who have struggled and worked righteous deeds (*'amal*), and while being amongst them, to rip off his clothes and expose his nakedness.'[12] The deeds are the clothes of the soul. This complex image requires a double perception. When in paradise, clothes are only figuratively the covering of the person; in reality it is knowledge because the afterlife is not physical. To rip off one's garments is a reprehensible act in and of itself; but it is also, by extension, the denial of faith by the repudiation of knowledge.

The correct course is to observe both faith and works. 'Whoever worships God, the exalted, by both means together and joins works to knowledge and preserves knowledge through works, that is a person committed to the command of God ... one obedient to Him and to His orders and prohibitions.'[13] This is enough to establish the strength and seriousness of al-Kirmānī's concern. In particular, his remark about someone who is of the Shī'a, and therefore among the *ahl al-janna* ('People of Paradise') and yet would cast off his outer coverings and reveal his nakedness beneath, conveys well the major purpose. He wrote this *Risāla* for his own people, the Shī'a, among whom there are some who hold to a doctrine that neglects or abandons the outward observances of religious law. They are wrong, he declares firmly, prior to outlining the correct path, one that ignores neither of the means to a proper appreciation (*ma'rifa*) of God but rather combines them both.

It is most significant, moreover, that al-Kirmānī wrote a treatise in which he bothered to argue not just the general principle but actually to delineate the specifics of the practical forms of worship. Unlike al-Qāḍī al-Nu'mān whose expertise was Shī'ī law and whose primary role was that of a judge, al-Kirmānī could not be mistaken for a legal specialist. Rather he was, principally, a theologian, trained in a different circle. But al-Kirmānī saw his function as involving both a gentle prodding of the official *da'wa* in the direction of philosophical doctrines he thought more sophisticated and therefore of greater precision – that is, away from some of those proposed by the earlier *dā'īs* such as al-Nasafī, al-Rāzī and al-Sijistānī – and, yet, at the same time, the promotion of an 'orthodoxy' that combined the best of the Ismaili tradition in a reasonable Shī'ī *madhhab* wherein neither the *bāṭin* nor the *ẓāhir* lost its place. To do this he avoided the more radical positions: on the one hand, by not dwelling on the esoteric interpretations of common rites and rituals, and on the other, by equating the *bāṭin* with knowledge, *'ilm*. Worshipping or serving by knowledge is, he says, 'recognizing what leads to the absolute oneness of God and the hierarchy of God's religion and comprehending the knowledge of their stations and ranks in such a way as to accord them their rightful due.'[14] For the *bāṭin* to be the intellectual component of faith, the *'ilm* or *'ilmiyya*, requires an important modification of at least some forms of the notion of *ta'wīl* and its significance. Nonetheless, al-Kirmānī chose this middle path – one less radical but more acceptable – and he clearly set forth in this treatise and others what he intended as the comprehensive statement of Ismaili doctrines. The 'Bright Treatise' is thus not a work of systematic theology, as is his *Rāḥat al-'aql*, but rather a pragmatic expression of those basic concepts and rules that constitute, in essence, the official doctrine of the Fatimid *da'wa*.

It should not be assumed, however, that this one treatise is unique in expressing al-Kirmānī's concern for the double observance and for the absolute obligation to perform all imposed acts and works that the law has ordained. The following passages come from three other works of his; two of them, the *Aqwāl al-dhahabiyya* and the *Kāfiya*, go back to the period prior to his arrival in Cairo. Both, moreover, were written to refute the doctrine of non-Ismailis, one the notorious Abū Bakr al-Rāzī, who believed that all humans possess the capacity for discovering scientific truths and do not require prophets at all, and the other the Zaydī imam, who had challenged the Ismaili concept of esoteric or *bāṭinī* knowledge. Thus, while the *Waḍī'a* may have been directed at wayward members of his own *da'wa*, these other works constitute a defence of the basic doctrine against its detractors everywhere.

In his *al-Aqwāl* the basic subject under discussion is medicine and the treatment of illness. Abū Bakr was, al-Kirmānī admits, a physician of admirable stature and justly famous, but he knew nothing about the diseases of the soul. He was thus utterly unqualified to write a book on 'The Spiritual Physick' (*al-Ṭibb al-rūḥānī*). Al-Kirmānī's view of the human soul was, of course, quite different from that of Abū Bakr, and his notion of how to effect a cure for its predicament involves a religious understanding of the condition of the soul and the way to achieve it.

> In the same way that God made medicines for the body in times of illness which might be used to uncover and be rid of it, He fashioned for the soul prescriptions which would be medicine for its illnesses and a means for it to recover its good health. These are His commandments, prohibitions and exhortations which attract and repulse, and the refraining from acts of disobedience and the things He forbids, so that through them the soul's deeds and actions would cause in its essence a desire that arouses it to adhere to them and the rest. ... Accordingly, God sent the one He chose from the realm of soul and delegated him as the Messenger to all mankind. We were singled out among them by the Key of Mercy and the Lamp of Guidance toward wisdom, Muḥammad, who issued a law for the souls in his community that combined the two laws in such a way as to conjoin the commandments, prohibitions and rites into an obligation and law, by making either licit or illicit things on account of which the soul would recover from its illnesses. These are the two forms of worship. One of them involves acts

requiring declarations by the tongue and works of the limbs and members, such as comprise the profession of faith, confession, purification, the call to prayer, the *iqāma*, prayer, bowing, almsgiving, fasting, pilgrimage, *jihād*, acts of obedience and submission to the Friends of God who were appointed to teach, patience and consistency in all these acts, to regard as lawful what is lawful and forbidden what is forbidden, and to be abstemious, devout, contrite and repentant. The second involves knowledge as envisioned in the essence and accepted in the heart and comprising cognizance of the beings that God brought into being as existents that precede the soul and function as the reasons and causes that regulate its coming into being: the nearest [cherubic] angels whom the Philosophers call the secondary beings (*al-thawānī*), and their essences, numbers, ranks and actions; and the highest heavens, their throne and footstool; and the planetary bodies and the bodies in the void that move, their ranks and the conditions of their visibilities, their locations and actions; and the bodies that are lower than these, such as the elements fire, air, water, earth, the minerals, plants and animals; and the prophets of God who were sent as messengers and their various ranks, and those who stand in their stead and preserve for the realm of soul its good order; and their adherents in it who are designated for teaching that through which it will acquire knowledge of the absolute oneness of God.[15]

In this passage the issue of esoteric knowledge does not appear, but it is clear that the second part of the law is intellectual, it is *'ilmī*, and is a part of what he often calls the observance by knowledge (*al-'ibāda al-'ilmiyya*) and which we observed earlier in the *Waḍī'a*. It is the *bāṭin*, the knowledge imparted exclusively by the *da'wa*, according to al-Kirmānī, and it ultimately derives from the Prophet and the imams, and not from any other source. It is simply not available to ordinary humans, even those like Abū Bakr al-Rāzī or the Zaydī imam, who otherwise have acute and proven intellectual talents. But it is, nevertheless, scientific in that it comprises science and the knowledge of the true reality of all beings.

Defending the *Bāṭin*

In answer to the Zaydī imam who had attacked the Ismailis for their doctrine of *bāṭin* and *ẓāhir*, al-Kirmānī lays out a careful but firm defence of the general principle that both are necessary and essential; they are indispensable. But, he quickly adds, there is nothing untoward or particularly mysterious about the *bāṭin* except how it must be learned. In the same context, and in midst of one of his most interesting discussions of the relationship between *bāṭin* and *ẓāhir*, he goes on to say:

> When we specify the *ẓāhir*, we mean by it the acts ordained in the law in accord with the subordinate parts of the profession of faith, namely prayer, alms-giving, fasting, pilgrimages, *jihād* and the implementation of the acts of submission to the person in authority, on whom be peace. All these acts and rites in the law which, when they come into being, are perceptible to the senses, are commonly perceived by every creature that possesses senses which are sound, as is the case with regard to the heavens, the earth, and what is between them of the planets, the elements, the natural kingdoms which, in that they are evident and obvious, are subject to sensation and every creature having sensation perceives them equally without any differentiation between one over another. If we specify the *bāṭin*, we mean by it the knowledge that accrues from knowing the existence of a thing and its elements and of its existing as a thing and whether it is manifest or hidden, of its measure and its form, of the cause of its existence, of the purpose because of which it has existence, which is a matter not subject to sense perception but is rather known by the mind, and of eternal punishment, the gathering, the reckoning, paradise and the inferno, the temporal contingency of the world and its annihilation, and other matters which, since they are esoteric (*bāṭinī*) in essence and hence are not subject to sensation, all groups do not participate in perceiving but instead one group is singled out to acquire it.[16]

The *ẓāhir* is obvious; all can comprehend it and perceive it. But the *bāṭin* is simply not readily apparent and is thus not accessible to all parties. It requires a teacher, a source of knowledge that is not available to humans by the very nature of being human. It was not given to them by the fact that they came to be. It comes instead from God's messengers and their successors, the imams, and it is propagated and taught by the *da'wa* acting on behalf of the latter.

Teaching and Instruction

'We admit,' says al-Kirmānī, in an important passage at the very end of his *al-Riyāḍ*,

> ... that the absolute oneness of God and an understanding of the hierarchy (of beings) is a truly difficult matter, but by means of it there is life for the souls and their eternity, and salvation from the world of nature and their ultimate transformation. Since it is so difficult, God knew that His servants as a whole would never achieve the level at which they could obtain a perfect understanding of God's hierarchy or of His own absolute unity. Therefore, God favoured among them all a single person in each age for that perfection and purity, as is the case with the imam, may God bless him profusely – that is, God favoured him with a perfection in which he receives completely the emanation that flows into the world of nature from the cherubic angels. This man is, by virtue of that emanation, guardian over them and their prompter toward all of that. God thus made obedience and love of him obligatory so that they will become, by virtue of that, a part of His following and thus the mercy and compassion from Him will be with them. There is no way to achieve that except by upholding the double observance (*al-'ibādatayn*) and carrying out the duties imposed in both knowledge and works, both the manifest and the concealed, and endeavouring to preserve them both. One cannot do that without being mindful of death and what follows separation from family, children, relatives and homeland, and of not being certain of reaching paradise without making provisions for it. But one cannot provide for it except what one accumulates through observing the imposed obligations, by duties fully carried out, good deeds properly done, pious acts accomplished,

and knowledge of the true reality of things acquired.[17]

To return to the content of the veneration by knowledge which al-Kirmānī equates here with the *bāṭin*, it is remarkable how theoretical it seems. Its subject matter is, in part, highly abstract and would, as he has just acknowledged, constitute a heavy burden on many segments of the general populace. In addition to fully comprehending God's absolute unity and oneness, the *tawḥīd*, it comprises knowledge of the angels, the prophets, their executors and the imams, and then, significantly, 'knowledge of the rank levels of the beings that have existence as they are in reality either intellectually or through sensation.'[18] It is thus quite apparent that the content of the 'scientific' or theoretical half of the service and veneration owed God is far more demanding than the compulsory ritual observances involved in religious practice. To insist, as al-Kirmānī does, that all believers must fully acknowledge both and that it is unacceptable for any to carry out merely the ritual acts without comprehending this other more intellectual side, also requires the existence of guides and teachers who will explain to the less gifted what they must believe.

The whole system, however, was carefully crafted in the beginning by the instigator of the law, the Prophet. He was the architect of the scriptural expression of the revelation, the *tanzīl*, which means, in the words of al-Kirmānī, 'to convey what had emanated on him of the blessings of the One in the form of revelation in as attractive expressions as possible, and to preserve it by creating a source for practical service (*al-'ibāda al-'amaliyya*) through rules instituted to function as a record that combines the essence of both observances at once, both knowledge and action, and as a treasury that preserves what is in it for its owner.'[19] The Prophet thus provides a law, a *qānūn*, which thereafter constitutes a source for those who teach, i.e. the *da'wa* whose role is to propagate and preserve the law. It is they who will explain both what practices must be observed and what concepts must be learned. They have therefore an obligation to teach and their function is one of *ta'līm*, to use the Arabic term. It is the law, however, to which the *dāʿī* refers in teaching the sciences:

> There must exist a law (*qānūn*) among the community that functions to provide a source to which those occupying the place of the Prophet may refer for the purpose of teaching, and that law is constituted by the book, the laws, regulations and edicts so issued.[20]

The system outlined thus far clearly requires a veneration of God that cannot be simply assumed. It must be taught. Its authority, moreover, is not casual. Even though the details of much of al-Kirmānī's sophisticated scientific explanations for the cosmos and creation appear to have parallels in the writings of persons who were not only not members of the *daʿwa* and indeed were often enemies of it, the aggregate whole, he would continue to insist, is uniquely the teaching of the imam. The law is thus preserved and explained by the living imam, above all. Beneath him the leading *dāʿīs* shoulder the responsibility of instructing the believers. None of this depends, however, on the transmission of knowledge from an older generation to a younger. The elders do not teach those who follow them, nor are any of them self-taught. The human soul commences its existence empty of knowledge like a blank sheet of paper. It then possesses no more understanding of itself and the universe than a wild beast. If, however, it finds the appropriate teacher, it begins to live a life independent of its body and its physical needs. The road to its salvation opens. At the end of that path is what al-Kirmānī calls its 'second (or ultimate) perfection.' That teacher is, after God Himself, the Prophet Muḥammad. Following him come the imams, one by one. All valid teaching therefore depends on the current imam and his appointed and fully authorized agents.

It is the *daʿwa* then that has the responsibility, acting on the inspiration of the imam, of explaining the law to ordinary believers and of teaching them both the practice of religion and its theory. Teaching is its *jihād*.[21] Their methods must conform to those employed originally by the Prophet. They will convert the abstract into a more accessible form. Teaching is also *ta'wīl*, the science of interpretation. It is to put everything that occurs in the visible realm into its real context, thereby providing life to what is otherwise dead. *Ta'wīl* is a second grace, a manna from God in relation to the first which was prophecy.[22] But those who teach 'are the experts in speaking, discussion, instruction, and representing the unseen by a thing that approximates it appropriately and in kind, and [which] gives an account of it in terms of what is closest to it in relation to the edicts and statements that came to the prophets from on high.'[23] Teaching is *ta'wīl* because it involves relating the law and the holy scripture, which embody theoretical truth as revealed to the Prophet, to the more accessible physical counterpart of it, which may be, accordingly, an outward ritual act or an obvious manifestation of physical reality itself, i.e. the visible world. The teacher begins with the most obvious and easily grasped things, such as models and pictures, and traces them back to their theoretical and abstract origin. But this process requires both procedures. To explain the abstract, the teacher must employ pictures and thus also move from what is theoretical and intellectually known down into a physical reality. Conversely, the student proceeds from the picture to the abstraction it represents. One is *ẓāhir* and the other *bāṭin*.

5

God, Creation and the Cosmic Order

To Serve God by Acquiring Knowing

The theme of the preceding chapter was al-Kirmānī's insistence on the doctrine of double observance in which service to God follows two courses: one practical consisting of acts, deeds and rituals, and the other intellectual or spiritual. The latter comprises the meaning behind the acts in the first set, but it also includes, most importantly, knowledge of the true reality of the universe and its created structure. Thus, for al-Kirmānī, God must be served and venerated by knowing as well as doing. Knowledge in this sense should be as comprehensive as possible, and yet it depends closely on having access to the proper sources of information. It is also both specific and general and it comprises the material of theoretical science as well as of religious revelation and its laws and scriptures. Again, it is al-Kirmānī's *al-Waḍī'a*, a manual of doctrine for the beginner, where the content of the 'worship by knowing' (*'ibāda bi'l-'ilm)* is most clearly delineated, as it ought to be given its fundamental purpose. There he also notes that, in terms of education and instruction, what is readily accessible is the more practical aspect of how one must perceive the universe as a whole. Practical matters thus come first in learning. The order of creation, however, is the reverse of teaching. It commenced with the highest and most abstract. It begins with extremely difficult theoretical principles and matters of forbidding complexity and ambiguity. Creation proceeds from God through the cosmic intellects and finally into the terrestrial world of physical existence. The realm of sensation falls at the end of this scheme, the lowest point in it, but also at the beginning of human comprehension. Start therefore, al-Kirmānī would say, with what is at hand, while realizing that the acts of daily observance should lead to knowledge of truths that have no direct connection to bodies or bodily being. Attaining fully developed knowledge is just as essential, perhaps even more so, as good deeds and timely acts of worship, for it is a worship in and of itself, and it will be the ultimate cause of the human soul's salvation.

It is thus obvious that one must find and acquire the knowledge that belongs to the 'service by knowledge.' There are a number of critical factors in this search but it depends primarily on the recognition and acknowledgment of its source. Again the key here is the concept of teaching (*taʿlīm*) and the institution that provides the only true teaching, the *daʿwa*, acting for and on behalf of the living font of all valid knowledge, the imam. He in turn derives his supreme authority from the Prophet and his Executor (*waṣī*), and theirs comes to them from the higher realm of soul in the persons of the angels who relay their knowledge down from God Himself. In part the knowledge needed by an ordinary mortal is what we would now see specifically as religion. It is contained in the sacred laws and in holy books that were revealed to and composed by the prophets, executors and imams of the past, many of which are still available. Most significantly, however, it also includes, necessarily, the living instruction of the current imam who alone provides validation for the writings and teachings of the past.

However, the requirement of knowledge does not end with religious doctrine as understood in the modern sense. It must, according to al-Kirmānī, include an understanding of the physical and metaphysical order in the cosmos, its science. In his 'Pure Treatise' he outlines carefully exactly what this latter aspect of 'service by knowledge' covers. It begins at the highest level with a thorough comprehension and appreciation of

God's absolutely unique oneness, the *tawḥīd*. In fact the whole cosmic system aims to instill this lesson. God is simply unlike any facet of the universe that He has brought into being. This is a concept, as will become quite apparent, which must be so rigorously observed that few have mastered it. Its metaphysics is formidable, even to the experts, and failures of comprehension abound among the theologians of Islam, the Philosophers, and even the eminent *dā'īs* of former times. One is allowed to wonder how mere common believers were ever to learn it correctly. Nevertheless, al-Kirmānī insists that the truth of *tawḥīd* must be both taught and learned. It is the ultimate aim and purpose of all instruction.

Next in the descending scheme comes acknowledgment of the angels, the prophets, the executors and the imams, followed by the books, laws, statutes and the application of interpretation to them – ostensibly a less scientific and more religious component. This aspect comprises the understanding of paradise, hell, resurrection, the judgement, reward, punishment and the Last Day which are matters that arise specifically from the teaching in the religious law. But beyond these the believer must also come to comprehend the nature of the existence of all beings that have come to exist. Here al-Kirmānī introduces concepts such as substance (*jawhar*), accident (*'araḍ*) and the categories (*maqūlāt*), using terms from the science of his day. He continues with physics or matters pertaining to physical existence (*al-ṭabī'iyyāt*). These include the methods of investigation by definition (*ḥadd*), division (*qisma*), analysis (*taḥlīl*), demonstration (*burhān*) and composition (*tarkīb*); the avenues of information from the five senses and terms like existing (*wujūd*), non-existing (*'adam*), place (*makān*) and movements (*ḥarakāt*). These two areas comprise chapters ten and eleven in his outline of what serving God through knowing must include. It would seem that they require courses in physics and metaphysics, but there is still more.

Chapter fourteen adds knowledge of how the existent beings are related and connected to each other, and chapter sixteen is specifically about the intellect (*'aql*), soul (*nafs*), prime matter (*hayūlā*) and form (*ṣūra*). Those in between cover the hierarchies and the obligation of allegiance to members of the hierarchy by loyalty and, most essentially, by an oath and covenant to them. There is no question but that an understanding of God's hierarchies (*ḥudūd*) and the beings that come to exist through His act of innovating (*ibdāʿ*) is obligatory on the believer. Al-Kirmānī emphasizes this latter requirement – that is to acquire a comprehension of the rank order of existing beings – by citing several verses of the Qur'ān, among them the passages which begin with the admonitions: 'Have they not considered the heaven above them, how We built it and adorned it, and there are no flaws in it,' 'So let man consider from what he was created,' and 'Do they not consider how the camel was made?'[1]

Thus a believer who reads al-Kirmānī's books and treatises could not escape being fully aware that he or she must at some point begin to acquire at least the fundamental concepts included in this intellectually challenging service to God. It is therefore of great interest, both historically and otherwise, to learn more of what he tried to teach about these matters and how he went about this task. Since we cannot recreate his oral instruction because we possess only his writings, and since his advice to begin at the most practical level is also hard to follow without having the appropriate teachers, it seems more useful to outline his intellectual doctrines more-or-less in the order of importance and commencing therefore with *tawḥīd*. But it also appears appropriate to extract the purely scientific concepts – those that would now be subsumed under the term philosophy – from matters more properly of religion, and to discuss the first separately in this chapter prior to bringing them all together in the next.

Tawḥīd

No doctrine is as central in Islam or as important specifically to Ismaili thought as *tawḥīd*, the declaration or attestation of God's absolutely unique oneness. Most theologians struggled with this concept, and they worried mightily about how best to express it. The problem of *tawḥīd* does not concern knowing God or proving His existence, but rather stating the fact of His oneness in such a way as to preclude any taint of duality. The Ismaili concept in this case is not a matter of knowledge of God; He is not served by knowing Him but, perhaps ironically, by acknowledging as completely as possible that He cannot be known. The objective is knowledge of *tawḥīd,* not of God, and the distinction between the two lies at the heart of al-Kirmānī's effort to protect the doctrine of God from being compromised by the imperfect processes of human perception and knowledge.

Al-Kirmānī's predecessors of all kinds devised various formulas to preserve the *tawḥīd.* Some were feeble indeed but, of those with credence, in the view of al-Kirmānī, three serve as a useful point of departure for the discussion of his own. The Mu'tazilīs advanced a long way toward purifying the concept of God's oneness and al-Kirmānī acknowledged their contribution, but he was also highly critical of their mistakes and their ultimate failure to pursue the course they began with full rigour. From another angle, the Philosophers spoke of a One that was the origin and first of all things, the cause of all causes, the first substance, the necessary being, the unmoved mover, and other notions in the same vein. Their analyses of what it means to be first, ultimate or necessary were obviously of help in solving the problem but, by conceding that God is the first being or first cause, the Philosophers located Him within and not outside the chains of beings or of causes. They would have God belong to and be a part of the cosmos. The earlier Ismaili *dā'īs*, most particularly al-Nasafī and al-Sijistānī, likewise attempted to define *tawḥīd* in such a way as to remove all residual duality and they, especially al-Sijistānī, perceived quite well how the Mu'tazilī theologians and the Philosophers were doomed to failure. They were prone to the error of thinking that their attempts to exclude God from comparison to His creation were not in and of themselves human conceptions of God. The very doctrine of God, as it appeared in the minds of these thinkers, was itself human. God was made thus into a human intellectual image – an image created by and for humans in which God remained a figment of their power to reason.

But, if al-Nasafī and al-Sijistānī understood the problem, they nevertheless could not solve it without recourse to ideas that al-Kirmānī found wanting and seriously inaccurate or imprecise. In the case of al-Nasafī, al-Kirmānī wrote a chapter in his *Riyāḍ* specifically to correct the errors he discovered in his predecessor's *Maḥṣūl* on this very topic. Al-Sijistānī was the subject of several small treatises by him, two of which constitute a rectification of doctrines advocated by the older master. For al-Nasafī, in the view of al-Kirmānī, one main difficulty was the use of terms that simply do not accomplish what, perhaps, the author had intended. Similarly, he says for al-Sijistānī language was a problem. There were, however, more intractable errors for both in that they had compromised the rigour of *tawḥīd* by asserting that God in one way or another directs His creation through a command and a will, and that this command or will occupies an intermediate position between God and the first being. This is the 'word' (*kalima*) of God and, although they characterized it as an entity 'not having existence' (*laysiyya*) it is, in their thought, nonetheless a distinct intermediate mediator and comes thus before being itself.

There are more details to this concept which was once fairly widely accepted by the Ismaili *da'wa*. Al-Kirmānī, however, rejected it outright and in principle because, in his view, it did not preserve the *tawḥīd*. For him there cannot be an intermediary between God and created being. No entity comes between the two. Earlier proponents of the doctrine of divine 'command' or 'word' tried to uphold this notion on the basis that it was not really an existent and therefore was only a quasi-entity. They would, moreover, have agreed with al-Kirmānī that once it comes to exist, it is not distinguishable from the first being or first intellect. For him, however, the seriousness of the subject demanded greater effort and, to amend the doctrines of all these predecessors, he set out to define his own doctrine with an even bolder approach that would avoid the mistakes of these other groups, including especially his own colleagues from the earlier *da'wa.*

Although the principle of *tawḥīd* dissuades humans from believing that they can know God because that implies that they somehow comprehend Him, despite His being above and beyond any such implication, this does not put God Himself in doubt and is not a doctrine of atheism. The Qur'ānic description of God remains valid, if properly interpreted according to the rules of reasoning. The existence of God cannot be denied; that He would be non-existent or have non-existence is impossible and absurd.[2] If the world exists, God is and must exist.[3] In his way of arriving at *tawḥīd,* al-Kirmānī will run through the proof offered by the Philosophers concerning the first being, first cause, necessary being (*wājib al-wujūd*), and then note that the resulting end of the causal series is, despite its primacy in that series, still a part of that series. This end is intellect, the first intellect, and not God. Nevertheless, the fact that God is beyond the first member of the series does not nullify His reality. He is that on which the series itself depends. All else contains or sustains duality; He is that by which contrariety becomes null or is finally absent. God is the very principle of existence. He is not an existent being but rather that on the basis of which first being has existence.

God is also not a substance as the Philosophers had held. To be substance, He would require a determining agent, and form and matter. A being must be either substance or accident, both of which would be absurd in the case of God and therefore for Him to be a being is simply impossible. Likewise He is neither corporeal nor incorporeal; neither potentially something (*bi'l-quwa*) nor actually something (*bi'l-fi'l*); He has no need; nothing is similar; He has no relationship, no contrary, no equal, is not in time and not subject to time, and He is not eternity nor subject to eternity.

Al-Kirmānī's point in all this is that God is utterly unknown and unknowable. As much as the intellect might want to grasp Him or to comprehend and understand Him, it cannot. To try only increases its distance from Him and fills in the space with confusion and false doctrines. God can no more be perceived by the intellect, even the universal first intellect, than the sun be seen by the naked human eye. To look upon the sun causes blindness.[4] He cannot be perceived by the methods of intellect such as the techniques of definition, analysis, proof, classification and demonstration.[5] To state that He is beyond intellect thus means exactly that for al-Kirmānī. Knowledge is intellectual and thus all perception of God is precluded by His not participating in the domain of intellect.

There remains, however, a feeling that it is only language that cannot bridge the gap and explain what God is. Qur'ānic terms seem properly to refer to God and to characterize Him and indicate His attributes. In fact it is the attributes of God that caused the earlier Islamic theologians such distress and controversy, according to al-Kirmānī. They did not realize that none of them validly apply to God. Languages cannot signify God as He really is, since the signifier must have a referent that exists and can be known. God, however, is unknown; one cannot signify with language or with abstractions in the mind something that is unknown. Therefore, one simply cannot speak about God despite recognizing that He is, nevertheless, there. His there-ness is indicated for al-Kirmānī by the Arabic term *huwa* and *huwiya* ('He-ness').[6] God is also unique (*fard*) and the instigator or innovator (*mubdiʿ*) of all creation. But these terms are largely directional rather than meaningful; they point vaguely but do not specify.

Following al-Sijistānī, al-Kirmānī advocates a process of double negation to purify the *tawḥīd*. At this point it has become obvious that a true *tawḥīd* tolerates no compromise, even of the most intellectually sophisticated and subtle kind. The proper procedure then is to deny all physical and mental images or concepts that seek to understand and encompass God. None are valid. After denying them all, this method goes back through them and denies the denial with a second negation. God is not in a place and *not* not in a place; He is not describable and *not* not describable, to use two examples. What this method achieves is the removal of God from the sphere of human speculation and imagination. It is a reminder that He is not susceptible to the operation of intellect, nor, in fact, to any human perception at all.[7]

But then where is the standard, religiously based, doctrine of God? Has al-Kirmānī not removed God altogether from human consciousness and made Him unsuitable for religious worship and service? Certainly al-Kirmānī did not believe that to be the case, but his doctrine at this point enters onto a perilous course. He himself knew that quite well. His answer is that what humans speak about when they talk of God is actually the intellect at its highest and ultimate first level. It is not really God and should never be confused with the true Lord Creator, but it is as close as humans can come. It suggests God but is not Him. Thus, if the God humans know and recognize is the first intellect rather than the real God, the authority for their understanding of the divine cannot derive from this intellect directly simply by virtue of how it represents God to them. But within the system itself, and built into it from the beginning, there exists an avenue of proper knowledge that flows down through the cosmos in a special channel to the bringers and bearers of revelation and religion. God is the Teacher par excellence. His cosmic system of intellects transmits His instruction and that ultimately reaches humans through the *da'wa* acting on behalf of the living imam. Alone and by themselves, human beings cannot know about God with any authenticity; but through the hierarchy of God's own devising, it comes to them as far as it is possible for humans to know Him.

In this concept of *tawḥīd* there are a number of interesting features that deserve comment. One is its astonishing rigour in rejecting all the compromises of the earlier theologians. God has in this system no attributes at all, for example. The double negation nullifies every approach, intellectual, perceptual or even intuitive. Humans do not and cannot know God except as the quasi-divine intellectual image present in the mind and it is not God. Yet this very notion of God as an ultimate first being or first cause is the doctrine of the Philosophers. It should be abundantly clear that al-Kirmānī rejected the philosophical concept of God as totally inadequate. God is beyond the cosmic system that He brought into being; it shares nothing with Him, nothing at all in any way. But in the end al-Kirmānī has allowed their notion of God back in with the reservations just mentioned. What remains thus looks quite like the account given by al-Fārābī, for example, and is not far from that of Ibn Sīnā. The God known to humans is the cause of causes, the unmoved mover and the necessary being.

Creation and the Cosmic System

Al-Kirmānī was and is justly famous for his advocacy of a new departure in the Ismaili teachings about the cosmic order. The contributions of al-Kirmānī to this subject are therefore especially interesting and noteworthy. They constitute certainly an important distinguishing feature of his thought. He was the first member of the Ismaili *da'wa* to recognize a system of ten intellects that function as intermediaries between the unknowable God and the terrestrial world inhabited by human beings. This notion was then most closely connected to the philosophy of al-Fārābī in whose writings it appeared for the first time in the Islamic context. Subsequent to al-Fārābī, it became more and more widely accepted; it was central to the cosmology of Ibn Sīnā, for example. But it had not been taught in any form by the Ismaili *da'wa* prior to al-Kirmānī as far as we can discern. Instead the system that prevailed within the movement was that first proposed by al-Nasafī and later refined and improved by al-Sijistānī. The works of al-Sijistānī had become a sort of standard by the time of al-Ḥākim and they were apparently read, copied and imitated by the *dā'īs*. Even later the ideas in them persisted and reappeared, as, for example, in the works of Nāṣir Khusraw, as if to confirm that al-Sijistānī's explanation of the cosmos remained the dominant school in Ismaili thought for a long time after al-Kirmānī. Yet, it is important to note that al-Kirmānī's view closely accords with that of the major philosophers of his time, whereas the system adopted by al-Sijistānī found little continuing popularity outside its narrower sectarian circle. Over the course of the fourth/tenth century it came more and more to be considered exclusively Ismaili. In fact by the period of al-Ḥākim, some opponents of the Ismailis regarded it as a subject of derision, almost an archaic quasi-science. In this view, the *da'wa* continued to follow the older doctrine in this area.

It is vital here to appreciate the various philosophical and scientific currents involved. Al-Sijistānī was, in these matters, a Neoplatonist who espoused doctrines about a universal intellect and universal soul that generally matched those of the ancient Greek founder of Neoplatonism, Plotinus, a portion of whose *Enneads* circulated in Arabic translation as the *Theologia* (*Uthūlūjiyā*). There were several other Neoplatonic Arabic texts available and they were all, without question, consulted and used by the Ismaili *da'wa*. In conformity to certain notions in this material, al-Sijistānī and other *dā'īs* of his period or earlier introduced a new version of an even older Ismaili cosmology in which God as the Innovator/Creator and intellect and soul play the key roles in creating and governing the universe. For these scholars, who were, after all, advancing ideas of quite profound sophistication, this teaching was then shared by numerous highly competent thinkers both within and outside the *da'wa*. There was nothing strange about it and it had had a long and distinguished history in Greek philosophy and in Christian theology.

However, with the work of al-Fārābī, who followed the philosophy of Aristotle almost exclusively except in his acknowledgment of the political thought of Plato, Neoplatonism ceased to stand its ground. In truth in its purist form it never achieved much of a hold in Islamic thought, despite the presence of the widely read *Theologia*. It had, however, already been adopted by the Ismaili *dā'īs* who continued to prefer it. Meanwhile, al-Fārābī, particularly in his political treatises, laid out a cosmic system that, although not found exactly in Aristotle, represented an interpretation based on his principles. Significantly, it does not have an identifiable Neoplatonic source although it is often said to be of Neoplatonic provenance. Most of its critical points simply depend on Aristotle and not on Neoplatonism.

In this new cosmology, God is the unmoved mover of Aristotle, for example. He is the first being, the first cause, the necessary cause of all causes; He is also the first intellect, the first of intellects. A series of intellects follow, each to govern a corresponding sphere of the heavens, leading at the level of the tenth to what al-Fārābī, after Aristotle, calls the Active Intellect which controls and governs the realm of earthly beings.[8] There are in this system ten intellects, but none of them is truly a universal intellect in the way that the Neoplatonic intellect is. The latter is universal both in transcending what is beneath it and in being immanent in the world; it is the intellect in humans; and it is the sum of all existents in this world and that. Most importantly, it does not break up into separate intellects and could not serve as the ten quasi-independent regulators of the spheres. Even more importantly, in al-Fārābī's scheme, there is no scope for a universal soul in the sense defined by the Neoplatonists, including al-Sijistānī. For the latter our souls are a part of a universal soul; al-Fārābī and al-Kirmānī will have none of this. In the scheme of al-Kirmānī, by contrast as will be seen, what he calls soul is merely second intellect and it shares nothing with the universal soul of al-Sijistānī. Human soul and second intellect, moreover, have little in common; and likewise first intellect is not the counterpart or partner of the human mind. It is not the sum of existent beings in any way.

But while these points are fairly obvious, the contribution of al-Kirmānī was not so simple as to be explainable by assuming his importation of al-Fārābī's Aristotelian cosmology and supplanting the older Neoplatonism with it. Neither al-Sijistānī nor al-Kirmānī accepted philosophy as a valid science as such. For them the Philosophers, even though gifted and astute, nevertheless relied exclusively, by their own claim, on the results of their personal investigations or that of their predecessors in philosophy. What they had discovered they advocated, but without authority and certainty. Ismaili thought, in contrast, derived its truthfulness directly from the prophets, their executors and the imams. As al-Kirmānī sought to adjust the Ismaili legacy and move it toward a new teaching, he must have had authority to do so from his own superiors. It is clear, nonetheless, that he felt he needed to bring together and harmonize both the newer system based in this instance, we can see, ultimately on principles taught by Aristotle, and the other, then current in Ismaili thought, which was derived from Plotinus. The two writers closest in time to al-Kirmānī were al-Fārābī, on the one hand, and al-Sijistānī on the other. Al-Kirmānī's task then was to insinuate the newer doctrine into an earlier Ismaili teaching without compromising the former or denying the important contribution of the latter; and above all to maintain and improve the programme of the *da'wa* in its role as the teacher of the knowledge necessary to serve God.

The first step in this adjustment was to insist on the doctrine of the unknowable God as outlined above. Al-Kirmānī followed al-Sijistānī in this quite closely and he avoided thereby subscribing to the Philosopher's notion of the divine. The God of al-Sijistānī and al-Kirmānī is not that of the Philosophers. Likewise God's primordial creation *ex nihilo* does not fit any of the ancient Greek concepts. It is not an act of emanating, a kind of causation that properly belongs to Neoplatonism, for example. To express the radical coming-into-being of the cosmos that God brought about, a number of Islamic thinkers resorted to the special term *ibdā'* from the verb *abda'a.*[9] It denotes a unique kind of creating that only God accomplishes which is to bring about something not from something (*lā min shay'*). It is not correct to see this act as making something out of nothing but rather literally 'not from something.' In other words, one cannot and should not categorize the prior situation by the term 'nothing' or 'nothingness' just as it was not 'something.' There is no nothingness without something; no-thing is the negation of some-thing, not a prior condition. In accord with al-Kirmānī's doctrine about the utterly unknown God, so too, with God's role as 'Innovator' (*mubdi'*) it is simply inexpressible and ineffable. The term *ibdā'* may quite properly be said to have no meaning except that once the cosmos exists, the intellect knows that its own existence depends on its having been brought into being. That knowledge is itself the *ibdāʿ* in so far as it can be known, and it is therefore an aspect of intellect, that is, of the first intellect which is the primary and most direct result of God's *ibdāʿ*.

This is a process that did not concern the Philosophers who do not recognize either the God or the 'innovation' outside of and prior to cosmic reality. But al-Sijistānī had admitted and advocated both doctrines. His troubles, however, began, in the view of al-Kirmānī, when he tried to mitigate the radical separation between God and the cosmos, between God and His creation, by acknowledging an intermediary, said variously to be the word (*kalima*), the will (*irāda*), the one (*waḥda*) or the command (*amr*). God creates by the action of *ibdāʿ* and it and the intellect are subsequently one and the same, but the intermediary nevertheless performs a role as the expression of God's will in determining that the cosmos should come to be. Such a doctrine was unacceptable to al-Kirmānī. It compromised the separation of God and brought Him back into a direct relationship with His creation. Al-Kirmānī simply denied any such connection and at several places in his writings he included a refutation of al-Sijistānī's doctrine.

According to al-Kirmānī, what came into being by *ibdāʿ* is the first intellect which is, subsequently, the absolute first of the cosmos: the first being, the first cause, the first mover. It is the one, the first cause and effect, the innovation and innovated (*ibdāʿ* and *mubdaʿ*), perfection and perfect, eternal and eternity, existent and existence all at once. It is the word (*kalima*) and it is the nearest angel (*malak muqarrab*).[10] Though one, it thinks, is thought, and is what is thought. Al-Kirmānī readily and quite pointedly characterizes the first intellect – i.e. the first being in the cosmic order – as the eternal[11] unmoved mover.[12] It causes motion by and of itself and needs nothing other than itself to bring this act about. Applying the Aristotelian model of the Philosophers, the unmoved mover is God, the cause of all causes. Therefore, recalling al-Kirmānī's recognition that this intellect serves as the God that humans know and understand, here he confirms the Philosophers' position, but with a profound and momentous change. The God of al-Fārābī and Ibn Sīnā is the first intellect as they would have said, but we know as well that it is not really God at all but an intellectual image actually unrelated to the real God. Significantly, the first intellect is not self-subsistent or self-generated, as it is in the view of the Philosophers, but is, rather, the product of another, the true God. It does not have existence by virtue of its own essence. Thus, although intellect cannot know God, it longs for Him, that Other, and as it does it realizes only that its own existence depends on a source which it fails to comprehend or understand.

This first intellect is nevertheless absolutely unique and one of a kind, although it bears some relationship to the cosmos which it now causes. It is the first thing of other things; the mover of all motions; and it is the actuality that brings all potentiality into actuality. There are, says al-Kirmānī, five kinds of intellect: a first, a second, and three types in the human mind – acquiring, potential and actual. The first is prior to all others and it causes all the others to submit to their maker. First intellect has three aspects or relationships: to that on the basis of which is its own existence; to that whose existence is based on it; and to its own essence. It is a principle that from God only one can come on the basis that from absolute one only one comes, but from the latter one there must be two. First intellect is one in essence but multiple in its aspects or relationships and thus it gives rise to a dual being, the second intellect, a being of more complexity than the first. The process of going from the first to the second broadens creation as it moves from the Preceder (*al-sābiq*) to the Secondary (*al-thānī*), from the Pen (*qalam*) to the Tablet (*lawḥ*), to use the special terms of Ismaili provenance, as does al-Kirmānī himself, at this point apparently in order to emphasize the continuity of his doctrine with the older versions. Most importantly, he now notes that the second intellect is otherwise called the soul as if to recall the universal soul of the Neoplatonists.

The second intellect arises from the first because the first unintentionally radiates its joy at being itself. It is so pleased and rapturous with its own being it blushes, thereby generating an image that becomes a separate second intellect which is like a reflection of it.[13] Resembling the reflection of something on the surface of water which would be that thing but only by virtue of a secondary effect, its *maf'ūl*, it comes to exist from the lesser aspect of its source. The process of its creation is called 'procession' or 'emanation' (*inba'atha, inbi'āth*). The second, in contrast to the first, has a rank and position in the very fact of its being second and thus not alone or unique. It is subject to procession; it is *inbi'āthī* rather than *ibdā'ī*, although, in so far as it is intellect pure and simple, it continues to have *ibdā'ī* qualities. It is actual and not potential; it is not moveable nor in motion, and it has no actions.[14] Yet it encompasses and preserves its own essence like the first. But, unlike its own immediate source, the second both must and can conceive from what it came; it envisions the first intellect as well as it contemplates itself, thus producing a double aspect which gives it its fundamental duality. In its imitation of intellect as agent, it is what al-Kirmānī calls soul – a soul, however, unrelated to human soul and clearly parallel to the universal soul of Neoplatonism only in name. The second aspect of the second intellect derives from the first in its capacity as effect. It now, in the second intellect, constitutes an intellect in potentia (*bi'l-quwa*) rather than in actuality (*bi'l-fi'l*). And, in contrast to the higher aspect, it takes on the characteristics of prime matter (*hayūlā*), an unrealized potential in which it, with form (*ṣūra*), produces bodily being. However, the potential intellect or *hayūlā* and the second intellect are really one and the same; they are together what he calls soul.[15] By itself the *ibdā'ī* aspect of the second intellect preserves its essence as intellect while, in its acquisitive mode, it is simply form to this material being but as a whole is potential life. The second intellect is thus both soul and prime, or more technically, hylic matter.

From the second then, in accord with its higher aspect, there issues a further procession of intellects and, from its lower, a parallel series of material entities. The former are the eight additional intellects of the cosmic system and the latter are the material forms of the spheres, out of which in turn the corporeal beings of the terrestrial world are generated as well. The outermost sphere is the sphere of spheres, the black dome of the heavens which moves in a westward direction relative to the rest, the second is the sphere of the fixed stars, and the third through tenth are the seven planets, all of which possess subtle bodies that are not composed of the same elements that make up earthly bodies. The material of the physical world is not the *hayūlā* of that higher realm. The bodies in these latter spheres move in an eastward direction.

Al-Kirmānī equates the seven celestial spheres and their governors with the seven heavenly letters but usually does not specify what the letters are. He does, however, assign to the intellects of these spheres the role of governing and regulating the physical world. They are intimately related to the progress of religious revelation and the development of sacred law. Each of these secondary intellects – called the *thawānī* by the Philosophers, he notes, in what must be a reference to al-Fārābī, observe their own veneration and service to God by their perfect unchanging circular motion. Its perfection is an emulation of or a desire for assimilation to the first intellect; its motion is like that of a pilgrim circumambulating the Ka'ba. They are arrayed in rank order, strictly determined by how many intellects precede. Each must acknowledge and attempt to comprehend all those before it; and this increasingly complex requirement burdens the next with an imperfection more serious than that of its predecessor. As the number increases, the complexity of the images required to comprehend those previous to each implies a certain need and impotence. But, nevertheless, relative to human society, the tenth intellect is the closest and most directly involved in the governance of terrestrial affairs and is thus the most important for it.[16]

The scheme of ten intellects which lies at the base of al-Kirmānī's vision of the cosmic realm almost certainly owes its basic expression and description to al-Fārābī who was the first to propose such a system in this context. However, some details do not match exactly.[17] In fact there are several interesting problems both in understanding precisely what al-Kirmānī intended and in correlating his scheme with that advocated by the Philosophers. An obvious difference is that for al-Kirmānī, God is not in the system at all; He is not the first member of it but rather outside it all together. Nevertheless, the first intellect has in a sense assumed the role of God, not in actuality as with the Philosophers, but figuratively. First intellect, for al-Kirmānī, cannot therefore correspond to any of the spheres; it is thus not the outermost sphere or *falak al-aflāk*. Clearly, the second intellect of al-Kirmānī would occupy the rank parallel to the furthermost sphere. It is a sphere which exists in a quasi-material form but lacks true bodily existence. Apparently, then, the first processive (*inbi'āthī*) being is the outer all-enveloping sphere of the observable heavens. Subsequently, the sphere of the fixed stars must therefore correspond to the third intellect. At this rank true bodily forms can be observed by the eye; the material of this heaven is real matter and belongs thus to the physical world which is apprehended by sensation. From here on there are seven planetary spheres: those of Saturn, Jupiter, Mars, the sun, Venus, Mercury and the moon. Parallel to each there is an intellect, because these celestial beings come into existence as the intellectual consequences of one intellect having an intelligence of its predecessor, and as intellect they correspond to the material entity that derives from their antecedent's lower aspect. To follow this scheme to the next step therefore requires that the tenth intellect also produces its own intellectual consequence and its own concomitant physical domain. The physical realm of the tenth intellect must be the terrestrial world wherein the hylic matter of the celestial bodies is now replaced with the elements that combine to form minerals, plants and animals. But what then is the earthly equivalent of the next intellect that, in this case, is only in the process of becoming truly intellect? It would constitute the eleventh intellect but it is, at present, not yet actually that.[18]

The roles of the second and third intellects loom rather large in this scheme. Indeed al-Kirmānī suggests that they are the

Human Soul and the Terrestrial World

A prime case in point is al-Kirmānī's concept of soul in the individual human being. He makes it perfectly clear that humans do not possess either a soul or intellect directly comparable to the celestial beings that are the first and second and which also can be called intellect and soul. Human soul is a substance found only in bodies and it does not have existence prior to the body in which and with which it acquires its being. Such a soul at the beginning is formless and devoid of knowledge although it is, nevertheless, the first perfection of its natural body. Intellect in this situation is a rational quality of the soul, a kind of soul, or more exactly, an aspect of it. Human soul and intellect are not separate entities or faculties in the individual. And neither soul nor its rational faculty can or will lead it out of its dependence on physical sensation for its knowledge of the world that surrounds it, despite this soul, as a substance, having the possibility of surviving its body.

The physical world is a creation of the forces described above as consisting of the ongoing procession of intellects and their corresponding material spheres. But in this realm prime matter is composed of combinations of the four natures: hot, cold, moist and dry; of the elements compounded of them, and the kingdoms of minerals, plants and animals which were produced out of them under the influence or agency of the planets. 'The four elements, the seven productive influences and the enveloping spheres all are the cause for the existence of what comes to exist beneath the sphere of the moon.'[24] As there are twenty-four permutations of the number four, so also are there twenty-four basic molecules of earthly bodies, and so on. Al-Kirmānī obviously had an interest in the details of natural physics and there is much more about this subject in what he wrote. But the main point here is that nature is a kind of perfection; it is the product of heavenly forces and the complexity of this realm is a direct result of the increasingly complicated variation in the celestial order which, despite its precise regularity, contains its own quite numerous permutations and combinations. In addition to the circular motions of the planetary spheres, for example, each comprises also a series of six lesser elliptic or retrograde motions that must be included to account for the way they move if the earth is assumed to be the centre of their various orbits.[25] Thus there are, he says, forty-two or even forty-nine separate motions in the heavens and the terrestrial events that correspond are at least as numerous as the factors of either of these numbers.

Human soul thus comes into being as the perfection of its body. In this beginning state, like nature, it commences with an instinctual comprehension of the surrounding world, exactly like that of the animal it is. Like other animals, it has life or the potential to live, but it also possesses potentially a possible second perfection, a purely rational existence in which its substance ceases to be attached to body and begins to live free and clear of it. Human souls, says al-Kirmānī, are at the lowest and most defective rank of any being that is non-corporeal. They are in body though not for its sake but rather for their own sake.[26] Although for the present they cannot exist without a body, that will not always be the case. Soul is 'a living substance with the ability, despite being devoid of knowledge at the beginning of the existence of its essence, of enduring beyond the dissolution of the material body, on the basis of what it acquires in the way of knowledge and good deeds.'[27] As a substance, its endurance depends on its essence and, although it was once without knowledge, it is nonetheless a locus for acquired understanding in being itself a substance. It will not decay or perish. And, since its very activity is connected to learning and knowing, its future must follow a like pattern.

This soul divides into three kinds or aspects of its single self: growth, sensation and rational discrimination. The third category is potentially intellectual. It also possesses six faculties: desire, estimation, imagination, cognition, memory and recollection. It develops through seven stages: conception, growth, sensation, imagination, rationality, intellectuality, and finally a 'second procession' (*al-munba'ath al-thānī*), the last stage being its final move from corporeal existence into an eternal state without body. Even with a rational faculty, however, it commences its existence without knowing what is in its best interest or what is good for it.[28] If it begins life lacking knowledge like, he says, a blank sheet of paper and thereafter undergoes a progressive development in which it assumes a different form, it in fact changes into something it was not previously. It is like raw iron which the smith forges into an object totally unanticipated and not evident in its first state.

At the start it is, from the perspective of true *ibdāʿī* and *inbiʿāthī* beings, sick and its illness is not due to its body but rather its own imperfection.[29] Soul is attached to sensation and on its own it cannot learn anything that does not strictly depend on information gleaned from the senses or extracted by induction from it. But, like the smith working with iron, there are intelligent forces that can deal with these souls and convince them to accede to the regimen that will bring them knowledge from outside.[30] They must have a teacher. If soul had possessed its own inherent ability to learn, it would not have its initial defect of being infatuated with the world of sense. It would have begun with a different orientation than the one with which it was born.[31]

As with celestial souls – the material forms of the spheres – human souls contain, however slight and weak they may be, some *ibdāʿī* and *inbiʿāthī* qualities. In a way they resemble distantly the intellect and soul of that higher world, and in turn that world preserves a remote interest in the souls of this realm. There is a similarity and accordingly the heavenly members of the hierarchy retain a providential responsibility for human beings. The world of soul in the larger cosmic sense is, according to al-Kirmānī, the spirit of holiness, the *rūḥ al-quds*, and it is that spirit which provides the impetus toward the second procession, the second *inbiʿāth,* for human souls.

The human intellect consists of three kinds, two of which it acquires and one given it at birth. The latter is a form of the material intellect, that hylic intellect, which is only potentially a real intellect. Al-Kirmānī calls this in Arabic the *ʿaql hayūlānī*, a term familiar from the writings of al-Fārābī and the other

Aristotelian philosophers. This is the intellect *in potentia* (*bi'l-quwa*) which may become an intellect *in actu* (*bi'l-fi'l*) if it receives what is necessary from the acquired intellect (*al-muktasab*). These three forms of intellect are directly connected to humans, unlike the *ibdā'ī* and *inbi'āthī* intellects which, however, share some characteristics with them. The difference is that the latter two act on other beings as well as themselves; they are agents that influence the beings beneath them. Human intellect, in contrast, operates solely on its own being and essence, with one major exception.

For the material or potential intellect of humans to move to a state of actuality, it must find and follow a teacher who can bring it the knowledge it lacks naturally. One important key is the tenth intellect of the heavenly world which has the greatest responsibility for the terrestrial realm acting on behalf of the whole system. It generates its own intellectual representative who, in turn, receives the emanations of all the higher angels, i.e. the separate intellects.[32] This person must be human but, as al-Kirmānī is careful to point out, it also must be someone who is *truly* human, a person whose human quality is most perfectly and exclusively intellectual and thus not merely animal. Only such a person actually resembles the angels in their *inbi'āthī* and *ibdā'ī* qualities. Such rare and unique individuals are in fact the *aṣḥāb al-adwār*, the masters of the ages, or in other words the great prophets and founders of religions on earth, and above all the messiah of the future who will finally represent the actualization of intellect among humans at the end of time.[33] Thus, for the present, the imam is the perfection of intellect in any one period; he is the ultimate teacher in this world because he most completely knows the truth. That is also why God is said to have created Adam in His own image (*'alā mathal ṣūrat nafsihi*), and why Jesus reported that he was the son of heaven (*anā ibn min al-samā'*).[34] These prophets were, in fact, the intellects of their time; they were the earthly image of true first intellect which is, as we have seen, God in so far as He is as an intelligible being.

Human soul thus must be awakened by fine exhortation

(*maw'iẓa ḥasana*) in order to stimulate in it a longing for its true second perfection and its ultimate salvation, a salvation based on its becoming, if not quite intellect pure and simple, at least the ultimate substance that it can be in its final, non-bodily form. For human soul, that is as close to an angel as it may become.[35] To see more clearly how this instructing of the soul comes about, we must now turn in the next chapter to the grand theme of al-Kirmānī's 'Comfort of Reason,' and the city of God on earth and in heaven.

6

The City of God

At the end of his career, al-Kirmānī returned once again to his major opus, a book that must have occupied him over many years and which quite likely had seen at least one earlier version. His new revision of it would be the final one and would subsequently become his masterpiece. We can only speculate about what it might have included in an older form or how his views about specific matters could have changed. All that is perhaps irrelevant. As it stands now it is possibly the most interesting and important work ever produced by the Ismaili *da'wa.* That it is the mature summation of a long period of investigation and thought is obvious enough and it deserves a great deal more attention from modern scholars than it has received.

The organization of the book alone is remarkable. Few works with a similar subject have a distinct plan that involves in and of itself a key principle in the scheme of doctrine. Most of them simply string together various topics without regard for overall coherence and their ultimate message, if one exists, is often lost or missing. In al-Kirmānī's *Rāḥat al-'aql,* by contrast, both the title and the controlling plan dominate. They convey in themselves the purpose of the book. *Rāḥa* is an Arabic word meaning 'peace,' 'comfort,' 'ease,' 'tranquillity'; it is the opposite of 'troubling,' and 'agitated.' The title thus has the sense of 'peace of mind,' 'comfort of intellect,' or perhaps 'assurance of reason,' and it implies freedom from the doubt and troubling confusion that go with life in a constantly changing and perennially unsettled world. It is this terrestrial realm that he is speaking about when he envisions for humans another life, the next life, a life of pure comfort, a comfort of mental peace and its pleasures which never stop. It is an eternal life of the mind. That then is the goal of his book as specified in its very title.

Al-Kirmānī intended to provide a complete guidebook that allows his reader to grasp and possibly understand exactly how to obtain that paradise of reason. But in many ways such a title and its implied aim is not unusual in either Islamic religious literature at large or in Ismaili writings. The purpose of the *da'wa* in general was the same. What is most striking about al-Kirmānī's 'Comfort of Reason' is that he sees the whole as a giant edifice configured on a cosmic scale into the image of a city which represents intellectually and physically the city of God. It comprises the universe and all that is in it, from the very image of God's own absolute oneness, through the celestial beings to the mundane world of minerals, plants and animals – all, of course, the creation of God Himself and therefore His domain as witnessed here as if it were a single urban habitat.

Al-Kirmānī is less than clear about the concept of this city as a city. Nevertheless the structure is obvious. His 'Comfort of Reason' has seven walls or ramparts (*aswār*, plural of *sūr*) and each 'rampart' yields or leads to seven internal pathways or thoroughfares (*mashāri'*, plural of *mashra'*). Only the seventh 'rampart' exceeds the strict plan of sevens since it contains an extra seven 'pathways' in order, as he himself implies, to complete the full circle and make it into the fortress it becomes when understood in its fullness. Conceptually, however, the individual pathways function more as topics that belong to various themes or subject areas and the ramparts act less like walls of a fortified city than divisions of a hierarchy. But the city that he wants his reader to envision, and the comfort which it affords the mind, is nonetheless evident from the simple outline alone. Gaining the ability to see the whole edifice brings that comfort and ease; it means the attainment of blessedness for our own intellects which are, at the moment, possessed of less than perfect souls which struggle now in the midst of the natural world.

The seven ramparts are the following: (1) the preparations necessary in order both to want to and be able to understand the book itself; (2) knowledge of *tawḥīd* and the method of glorifying God; (3) what the first existent being is; (4) what exists by procession because of the first being having come into existence; (5) what exists because of the latter namely nature and the celestial bodies; (6) what exists because of the celestial bodies, meaning here the mundane bodies of the terrestrial world; and finally, (7) what exists because of the higher and lower bodies as the kingdoms of minerals, plants and animals and, in particular, the human animal and its circumstances and ultimate perfection. (For a complete summary outline of the book, see Appendix C). Significantly, the final rampart comprises seven pathways that cover the development of animals and seven more on the condition of human beings. The whole is, in effect, a comprehensive summation of what the believer must know in order properly to serve God in accord with the requirement of the double observance. In order to know the things that exist as they truly exist, to obtain salvation and the ultimate comfort of reason in an eternal life as a consequence, this knowledge is exactly what is required.

That the mind is a city of knowledge is an old concept. Al-Kirmānī speaks himself of paradise as the city built by the prophets, the executors (*awṣiyā'*) and the imams. It has seven gates all leading inside to a wonderful palace full of luscious gardens and splendid rooms which are inhabited by countless angels.[1] The city of mind was also well known from some fragments of Plotinus's *Enneads* in Arabic, the so-called 'Sayings of the Greek Sage.' But the image most likely in this instance is that of the famous *ḥadīth* in which the Prophet Muḥammad said, 'I am the city of knowledge' and went on to add, 'and 'Alī is its gateway; so let whoever wants knowledge enter through its gate.' Al-Kirmānī himself quotes this *ḥadīth* in a number of places.[2]

Training the Soul

To this point it is clear that one preliminary purpose of the understanding to be acquired in the city of God is the realization that the cosmos has members that exist in a permanent state and others that fall under constant generation and corruption. A basic orientation is needed; the individual must comprehend the actual condition of his or her soul in relation to either or both of these realities. A body in this terrestrial world cannot endure; it is mortal and will decay back into the elements and natures that combined to engender it in the first place. The mind – its reason and intellect – resembles faintly the celestial intellects and, to the extent that it might emulate the way they are, it too may acquire characteristics that will assimilate its being to theirs. It – that is, the individual human soul – must somehow become intellect pure and simple; it must acquire an eternal form, a form like that of the angelic intellects. But, in the present, it can only anticipate and plan for what will happen when its body dies. Still, to neglect that eventuality will doom it to failure and perdition. The soul is currently beset with a sickness caused by its devotion to corporeal sensations and desires. Such a condition is natural to it, however, since it inhabits the abode of physical existence. But once that state is properly perceived, the mundane realm can be grasped for what it really is. Although the body is a necessary instrument of the soul and is indispensable, it should not predominate, and the soul, despite its sickness and inclination to indulge the body, must not allow itself to become devoted to its material side. In order to prevent or to control that tendency, the soul needs a restraining regimen that will both teach it to resist the temptations of the physical world and incite it to aspire after the knowledge that is proper to its real human self as a human and not as an animal.

Nevertheless, the body cannot be abandoned as long as it remains the vehicle of the soul. This earthly realm is an abode of acts and deeds and the body requires its own regulation and training. The first necessity of the soul's orientation is to learn how to care for the body in an orderly way and to habituate it to aid rather than oppose the good life, to bring the body into partnership with the soul, and thereby to provide the soul with the freedom to follow its higher calling. It is as if the soul were travelling across a sea in a boat; the boat is the means to its salvation, though not the salvation itself. But to neglect the sound upkeep of the boat or fail to steer it in the right direction will doom the soul as surely as to try to traverse the ocean without a vessel at all.[3]

What is critical in all this for al-Kirmānī is that the soul on its own possesses no better sense of direction or more information than that granted it by virtue of its first creation as a part of the natural world. Its nature is that of an animal that speaks and has some knowledge of how to defend and feed itself. It is not intellect and it does not have knowledge beyond these basic instincts. And, most importantly, even though required for its eventual survival, it does not have a means to obtain such knowledge. It cannot learn without a teacher, to repeat a theme that is so basic to al-Kirmānī that it constitutes the foundation of everything that follows. Even prior to approaching the gateway, the soul must first acknowledge the very necessity of entering into the city of God.

The *ḥadīth* quoted above provides a clue both to what stimulates the soul to seek knowledge and also where to find it. The Prophet has said that he is the city of knowledge and therefore the religion, the law, the *sharīʿa*, the scripture and all the regulations laid down by him, serve to awaken the soul and commence its training. He specified as well that the gateway to the city is his executor, ʿAlī, who instigated the teaching of that knowledge to others. Each had a different role but both participated in receiving the divine inspiration which came to them from the celestial angels. The Prophet's position is, of course, more complex and complete. He received the benefits that emanate from the heavenly intellects and turned them into a written law; he was, in fact, the lawgiver, the *shāriʿ*. The Prophet's knowledge is thus unique and not shared by ordinary human souls. 'The soul of the prophet, being a part of the world of religion, is distinct from all the souls of humans in its ability to receive the emanation (*fayḍ*) of the world of *ibdāʿ* from the direction of the first intellect with reception so complete that no other soul can equal him in it.'[4] 'The recipient, in his receiving that emanation, assumes the place of God, the Emanator, in providing instruction and guidance. The transmission of the emanation is the sending of the prophets and the recipient of the emanation is the prophet.'[5] He 'receives the emanation that flows throughout the world of nature on behalf of the nearest angels.'[6] 'The prophet is the summation of all excellence and the preserver of every benefit and fine manner and of good and comely habits, and he is the furthermost limit of the world of soul toward which every soul aspires, and he emanates these qualities to the others in that realm with mercy and spirit and holiness.'[7]

It should be noted that, in each of these passages that explain the role of the prophet, it is the emanation of spiritual holiness which provides him his unique powers and knowledge and, in each case, al-Kirmānī uses the Arabic word *fayḍ* (emanation). He denies the philosophical concept of causation by emanation except in this instance. It has then here a special meaning. It is perhaps related closely to the term *ta'yīd* from which derives the concept of the prophets as the *mu'ayyadūn*[8] – those who are infused with the holy spirit, the *rūḥ al-quds*, as the Qur'ān states explicitly in regard to Jesus. In fact the prophets possess a kind of knowledge that al-Kirmānī calls *'ilm ta'yīdī*, knowledge that is 'inspired,' as distinct from another kind which he says is *'ilm ta'līmī*, the knowledge by instruction.[9] Prophets have a special faculty that allows them to formulate and express what they know in a form which is directly accessible to those in the physical world. There is in this talent a prophetic art[10] that creates images and parables out of intellectual abstractions. The emanation from the celestial angels does not really suit the material world except in that it symbolically represents the true nature of the heavens and the reality of the higher realm. Nevertheless, out of it the prophet must fashion a comprehensive law, a *qānūn*, that will convey as much of that truth as is possible. 'In decreeing his regulations (*sunan*) and the laws (*qawānīn*) that he legislates (*shara'a*) he follows the method of providing indications of these obscure matters,'[11] i.e. 'the principles governing innovation and procession which are not available to the senses.'[12] Most importantly, that law ought to reach most, if not all, humans. Because their souls are born ignorant and devoid of the knowledge about what is best for them, his task is made difficult by their natural inadvertence. Thus, the aim of the law is not to teach those who want to learn but to instill acceptable behaviour and proper social norms in a society of unwilling and heedless members who may prefer to resist.

A good example of the knowledge of prophets is their ability to comprehend the order, arrangement and long-term movements of the heavenly spheres. Astronomy is a prophetic science in the sense that the prophets bring knowledge of it; they alone can explain it, even though it has now been taught to and by many others.[13] A second aspect of such knowledge is that the prophet also comprehends how to instruct the others by creating a way for ordinary humans to picture something they can barely see and only remotely understand, if at all. The Ptolemaic model of the universe is, according to al-Kirmānī, a digest of information gleaned from earlier prophets. But a more serious concern of the prophet is how to construct an effective model or representation of paradise and hell. It is like trying to show the fetus in the womb of its mother what the world will be like when it emerges into it.[14]

Revelation is in fact the emanation of the holy spirit or true soul to the prophet. As al-Kirmānī says: 'as regards revelation [*waḥy*], it is a name for what he apprehends in a general way without explanation or detail, and it is further divided into two categories, one of which he apprehends without an intermediary and the second he learns through a sensed medium.'[15] The prophet sees things others cannot see and he infers as well from the physical world by analogy. Prophets have the power to receive representations of intellectual forms and to retain them; they have souls that grasp the universal intelligibles and the particulars at certain moments; and that happens without cogitation or reflection and when awake and not in sleep.[16] With this power they express reality – even the abstract and hidden reality of divine matters – with unerring exactitude. The visual image, the law or the symbol they choose matches its original and the correspondence is perfectly apt, in contrast to the false language or fake icons of those who, like Daysān or Ibn al-Muqanna‘, are only pretenders to prophecy.[17] The statements and regulations – the laws and books – issued by the prophets compel humans to use and follow them. By so doing the individual souls begin to be transformed by the prophet's art like gold smelted away from the natural impurities with which it is normally found.[18]

The law-giving prophets are few in number. They started with Adam who was the first to formulate a law, a *sharī‘a.* Next came Noah, the first to abrogate one law and replace it with a better; then Abraham who was the first to perfect religion. Moses thereafter renewed the law of Adam; Jesus that of Noah; and finally Muḥammad that of Abraham.[19] Our era is that of Muḥammad, the seal of the prophets. It is his law that must be observed until the Day of Resurrection.[20] The whole historical progression, however, has as its ultimate aim the transformation of human soul into a form that is actually and authentically intellectual, a state in which it will endure eternally, like the celestial angels. The final messenger and representative of the world of soul is, therefore, the messiah who ushers in that last perfect day.

Meanwhile, in the absence of either the last messenger or of the coming messiah, reason demands that human souls have access to the knowledge they require for that final perfection and salvation. If they cannot seek their own way to God because the knowledge is not available to them by the very fact of being human, then it behoves God to appoint someone to guide them. 'It is necessary for Him, in so far as He is the All-wise, that He appoint in this world someone whom He teaches, and by means of the emanation inspires and makes a teacher and guide for the soul to that which will yield its perfection.' 'He must appoint someone to represent Him in instructing them, a person to guide them in His stead.'[21] The argument of al-Kirmānī then is that, because this knowledge is particular and not general and exists only in the chosen few, teaching is a necessary function of God, first, and of His appointed deputies, second. That explains, in the first instance, prophecy as lawgiving but it also imposes a continuing obligation. At the death of the law-giving prophet, someone else must perpetuate his teaching. He was a teacher in addition to a legislator. If he had not been both, the true meaning of his work would have disappeared with his death and the only facet of it that would survive is the external, literal and mechanical practice, the observation of works through ritual and good deeds, but only that. Both the basic reason for these acts and the rest of service by knowing would slip away as it gave rise to variations and deviations.

The first task is that of the executor, the *waṣī*, who institutes the very requirement of the double observance and regulates both the practical and the theoretical by his ongoing, living teaching.[22] He, in fact, creates the *da'wa* that is to sustain and propagate the truth brought by the lawgiver. His purpose is to instruct and to preserve; he is to guard the sacred message from defilement. Above all he is to explain what the lawgiver's ordinances and parables mean.

There is a danger in depicting law and religion in terms of accessible physical symbols and images. Its primary purpose after all is to have humans believe that which they ought truly to believe, to understand reality as it really is, and not mere phantoms of it. Souls mired in the physical world can think only by applying the tools of sensation; they need concrete material representations of everything spiritual. That is why the prophets are themselves pure of soul. They do not live for this world and therefore they can more easily gain access to that higher, non-material realm. But to instill the desired objectives in common people, it is necessary to convert the abstraction of spirituality into a physical approximation of it. Its actual purpose must, however, never be abandoned. The prophet's executor has the responsibility of founding the organization that will maintain that aim. To do so he begins by teaching its explanation, its *ta'wīl*, to those who continue to adhere to the true cause of the law-giver.

Inheriting from both the lawgiver and the executor, an imam preserves as much of either function as possible. Only he can know the precise teaching of either one; he is their child and their heir, both literally and figuratively. From them he inherits the authority of a lawgiver, which corresponds to the outward aspect of the religion, and that of the founder of the interpretation 'like the child that inherits from his two parents.'[23] This is not to say that he composes scripture or makes laws but rather that he, and only he, is the preserver of them.[24] He is their keeper. And below him there is a small army of assistants arrayed in ranks, each with its own special function. The scheme is in fact quite elaborate. The obligation to teach and to guide the people who worship God by the double observance of acts and knowledge is complex and 'it requires an abundance of providential attention from the supreme hierarchy.' A lawgiver must legislate laws, a founder must explain and expound them, an imam must preserve them, a *ḥujja* must teach them, a *dā'ī* must appeal to and create a desire for them.'[25]

Here then is the hierarchy of the earthly realm, the *ḥudūd*. In this case it has, as al-Kirmānī says, five ranks: lawgiver, founder (executor), imam, *ḥujja* and *dā'ī*. Balancing it in the celestial world are five as well: Pen, Tablet, Gabriel, Michael, and Isrāfīl, and thus in total, between the believer and what he worships, there are ten intermediaries, five above that are intellectual or spiritual and five below that are physical.[26] For the *ḥujja*, a word meaning 'proof' or 'assurance', it is hard to assign an exact function other than, as he says, to teach. In one place al-Kirmānī, who was said himself to be a *ḥujja*, states that 'the *ḥujja* participates with the *bāb* in accessing the inspiration which derives from the radiance of the imamate.'[27] The *bāb* seems to be a single 'gatekeeper' at the head of the *da'wa* to whom the twelve *ḥujja*s report. Khatkīn was the *bāb* and al-Kirmānī was a *ḥujja*. Below the *ḥujja* there are numerous *dā'ī*s who also have the responsibility of teaching. When an individual *dāʿī* does not know an answer to a problem, however, he consults the *ḥujja*. Those beneath learn from those above them. At one point in his *Rāḥat al-ʿaql*, he provides a complete list of the ranks in the *daʿwa* and the specific duties of each. They are the following: lawgiver, founder, imam, *bāb, ḥujja, dāʿī al-balāgh, dāʿī muṭlaq, dāʿī maḥṣūr, ma'dhūn muṭlaq, ma'dhūn maḥṣūr* and *mukāsir*.[28]

Al-Kirmānī's account of the hierarchy and its functions offers an unusually complete picture of it, although much of what he says is partially disguised in the standard *mīzān al-diyāna* ('balance of religion') – a type of exposition that he favoured. In it, as he frequently does for other matters, he reveals the details that interest us only through an elaborate series of correspondences, usually of the form, 'just as in this realm, such and such is true, so also must this other have the parallel structure as follows.'[29] A hierarchy in the celestial realm which contains ten members means that its counterpart on earth likewise must have ten ranks. There are innumerable examples of a similar kind in Ismaili literature and, in particular, this form of exposition permeates the *Rāḥat al-ʿaql*. Still it provides more information about almost any subject of interest to al-Kirmānī than any other of his books, including here the details of the hierarchy that ran the *daʿwa* in his time.[30]

This elaborately established hierarchy had a single purpose which was to convey as much benefit to the believer as possible. Without it individual human souls would be lost and adrift. Their own inclinations had to be based solely on what al-Kirmānī recognized as its first perfection, a natural state that it possesses merely as the animal it is. That state is, however, devoid of the true form that might separate it from the other animals and from its dependency on a material existence like theirs. Acceding to the *daʿwa* brings it a kind of knowledge that produces in it a form like that of the beings which do not require a body to exist. The instruction of the *daʿwa* calls for loyalty not only to itself as the rope of God – the one leading from a single believer all the way to Him – but to each member in it. Thus the entire earthly *da'wa* requests loyalty to the reigning imam, to the prophet of the age and his executor, to the angels of heaven, and to God Himself. In reverse order the grace of all those above flows down to the lowermost member at the bottom.

The message is that grace is a commandment to observe the rule of ritual acts and good deeds, to habituate the soul thereby to obedience and service, and to accustom it to the ethical and moral principles that govern a just human society. It also constitutes a demand to learn what the universe really is, what makes it and how, what are the rank orders of being in it, and what is the true position of humans. It is necessary thus to know about the first intellect, the second intellect, the origin of theoretical matter, and of the material in this terrestrial world, to understand that humans are the final stage and end of nature, and that the aim of the whole is to transform the potential intellect into a real and actual intellect. The higher order beings thus act as the outside resurrecting force which provides the controlling and guiding programme for the soul, once it has acknowledged its true potential self and grasped the principle that it is different from that with which it began.

This programme is in fact the *jihād* of the soul. The Prophet said that 'the striving of the soul is to restrain its natural impulses; its restraining them is its adherence to the service to God in accord with the rules issued and the regulations of religion and acting in accord with virtuous good behaviour. This is the more difficult *jihād*. *Jihād* done in this way ennobles the substance of the soul.'[31] The individual soul thus acquires fine and beautiful characteristics that it did not have; it is clothed in good deeds and truth. The soul is a seed and, as such, it grows under proper care into something that does not have the same form as that original seed. And, in the process, it begins to take on a form that will not disappear.[32] 'We maintain,' al-Kirmānī says, 'that the souls have the nature of those things that are separate, whose existence is an *ibdā'ī* existence, but neither its manifestation nor its existence takes place except out of the two worlds, the natural and the processive. It is a natural power that it obtains on the basis of what it acquires from the hierarchy by service and the double observance. Accordingly, there issues from its essence a form that is eternal and independent and which resembles the things that are independent in the next life, and yet it also differs from them in that respect and so we call it a second procession (*munbaʿith thānī*).'[33]

Just as the human being was created once, so too will the soul be subjected to a second creation in the future. The goal of the *daʿwa* is, therefore, to perfect the aspect of soul which will survive. This is an acquired perfection and not a natural one. It must be achieved by first educating and training the soul to resist the demands of nature and its bleakness, and second to conceive in it a knowledge of divine things and to give it the form that signifies angelic being.[34] 'The human being possesses a double aspect: one side belongs to the natural world and the other has divine qualities. The human therefore is neither the fruit of this world alone nor of that world but rather of both together.'[35] The task of the *daʿwa,* therefore, is not simply to release the inner spirit but to mould out of the existing human being a second perfection. The hierarchy exists to preserve the law, to spread its hallmarks, propagate its signs, and appeal for knowledge and acts; thereby and on account of this, humans are truly human. In this world the soul must think or cogitate but thinking as such does not exist there. 'Thinking does not have an existence separate from soul but is rather the essence of soul and will not endure by itself. For all of soul's acts, there is a cause for which it needs to act because of its being in the world of nature. When it separates from it, these acts cease to be and what endures eternally is only that essence which has acquired the form of pure intellect.'[36]

The last passage hints at the real state of the final version of soul. Soul departs from the body and lives on, divorced from both its own body and the world of nature. In some measure, it has become an intellect. The extent of its success depends obviously on its acquisition of knowledge. Once there the deeds and acts of its former life no longer count; neither do its previous thoughts and memories in so far as they related to that existence. Only the truth, only the knowledge of eternal things, of God and the intellects, lasts and stays with it. Its reward and its paradise resembles that of the perfect beings in the heavens, the angels.[37] It has eternal life like theirs and its rank, though not equal because it has no agency over others but only over itself, is possibly similar, depending, of course, on the degree of its knowledge.

That is the status of the soul at the death of the body. Upon the advent of the master of the seventh great age, in this case the messiah, a change occurs. Then the total sum of the emanating benefits will accrue to the one final inspired instrument of that world and, through him, God will complete the course of creation that none of those inspired messengers who preceded him had the power to accomplish fully. He will combine in himself all the radiance that emanates from the world of sanctity. At this ultimate moment God will create again, this time a new spiritual creation, and it will subsist thereafter on its own, worshipful and devoted in its material essence and sanctifying in its action. Like the seven celestial planets, it will then arrive in the world of holiness, of paradise, free at last from the restricting chains of earthly materiality.[38]

Appendix A

Al-Kirmānī and the Philosophers

In this study of al-Kirmānī and his work, we have looked as carefully as possible, given the surviving evidence, at the relationship between him as a thinker and member of the Ismaili *da'wa* and his imam, al-Ḥākim, as the ultimate source of knowledge and authority. We observed that the centrality of the imam appears obvious both in the dedications of his books and treatises and in the internal theoretical explanation of doctrine.[1] Al-Kirmānī also cited several of the earlier *dā'īs* as valued contributors to an enterprise he professed to share in common with them. Two in particular, however, al-Nasafī and al-Sijistānī, were mentioned by him with some ambivalence; he clearly felt a need to credit them for their efforts but also to challenge certain details in what they had said. Nonetheless, except to recognize that differences with them did exist and were a matter of discussion in his writings, it has not been possible here to review all facets of the arguments involved in his dispute with these figures. While some of the issues came up and were analysed, others could not be examined as thoroughly as they deserve without a lengthy prior investigation into the reasons for al-Sijistānī's (or al-Nasafī's) original position and then al-Kirmānī's rejection of it.

But another group that provided a major source of ideas for al-Kirmānī needs additional comment even in this relatively brief introduction to his thought. They form what he terms simply the Philosophers (*al-falāsifa*) without, it would seem, naming specific persons that he might include in this category.

Yet, despite this ambiguity about who they were and also his expressed general rejection of them and their doctrines, we can see quite well that his thinking depended heavily on the philosophical tradition and its proponents at many points. The philosophy in al-Kirmānī's work is highly important in and of itself, quite apart from his activities on behalf of the *da'wa*, and it alone makes him an exceedingly interesting and somewhat unusual figure who deserves to be the subject of scholarly inquiry for that reason alone.

Although not named, the key Philosopher in question has to be the famous Abū Naṣr al-Fārābī, who died in 339/950. A would-be philosopher, the physician Abū Bakr al-Rāzī, who desired to be accepted as a philosopher but was hardly ever recognized as one was, for al-Kirmānī and other Ismaili writers of the time, the object of considerable hostility on intellectual and other grounds. There is thus no chance of direct influence from him to them; and it is doubtful that al-Kirmānī included him among the Philosophers. The earlier proponent of philosophy, al-Kindī, may have had some remote connection – and could more likely have been regarded as a Philosopher – but, if he did, it hardly shows. He was much too early. With al-Fārābī the situation is, however, completely different and the lines of influence are unmistakable.

Al-Fārābī was the foremost representative of philosophy in the Islamic world prior to al-Kirmānī. He stands out as a kind of philosopher's philosopher and, in fact, it is quite reasonable to credit him with actually founding a school of philosophy. His interpretation of what philosophy is became, soon after him, the philosophical standard for all subsequent discussions about philosophy and philosophers. Thus when al-Kirmānī speaks of the Philosophers, he surely means al-Fārābī, even if he does not mention him explicitly by name.

The connection, however, goes much deeper. Al-Fārābī was properly famous for his writings on logic and his advocacy of its use. In line with that emphasis he was also a champion of Aristotle, the widely acknowledged 'master of logic' (*al-ḥakīm fi'l-manṭiq*), to use al-Kirmānī's own way of referring to him.

But, in addition to extremely important commentaries on the logical works of Aristotle, al-Fārābī wrote on philosophy itself – its history and development – and, most notably, on political philosophy. In these treatises he recognized the contributions of Plato but again admitted that the ultimate stage of philosophical achievement belonged to Aristotle.

The books of al-Fārābī in which he expressed his views on the role of philosophy in human society include his two most important political treatises, 'The Opinions of the Inhabitants of the Virtuous City' (*Ārā' ahl al-madīna al-fāḍila*)[2] and 'The Political Regime' (*al-Siyāsa al-madaniyya*),[3] plus 'The Attainment of Happiness' (*Taḥṣīl al-sa'āda*) which constituted the first part of a longer work on 'The Philosophy of Plato and Aristotle.'[4] These are not the only works of his to deal with aspects of this subject, but for the present purpose they are sufficient to indicate the seriousness of the relationship in question. Moreover, both the 'Attainment of Happiness' and 'The Opinions of the Inhabitants of the Virtuous City' exist in complete English translations; the 'Political Regime' is also available in English but only the second half. It is the first half of this work as well as of the 'Virtuous City' that contain an account of the cosmic scheme of ten intellects and how they unfold, one from the other, which so closely resembles the same system as expounded by al-Kirmānī. There are differences, but the similarity of the two is far more striking, even in the details, including the terminology, than are the disparities. Moreover, we have no other source in the Islamic world for this theory of ten separate celestial intellects which is clearly prior to al-Kirmānī.

The connection in this instance is all but certain and there are other matters that deserve to be investigated as well. The Belgian scholar Daniel De Smet looked at many of these issues in specific detail in his highly important study of al-Kirmānī; he notes and discusses the relationship in this case and his contribution is an extremely valuable beginning. There are, however, other factors as well, not merely matters involving the intellects, including al-Kirmānī's understanding of the imamate and his theory of instruction, both of which can be made to look as if they owe a good deal to al-Fārābī. Nevertheless, this is not the proper occasion to belabour this point beyond suggesting some interesting and tantalizing resemblances.

To do so, in brief, it may be enough to quote the following statements from al-Fārābī's 'Attainment of Happiness':

> ... the idea of imam, philosopher and legislator is a single idea. However, the name philosopher signifies primarily theoretical virtue. But if it be determined that the theoretical virtue reach its ultimate perfection in every respect, it follows necessarily that he must possess all the other faculties as well. Legislator signifies excellence of knowledge concerning the conditions of practical intelligibles, the faculty for finding them, and the faculty for bringing them about in nations and cities. ... The name king signifies sovereignty and ability. To be completely able, one has to possess the power of the greatest ability. His ability to do a thing must not result only from external things; he himself must possess great ability because his art, skill, and virtue are of exceedingly great power. This is not possible except by great power of knowledge, great power of deliberation, and great power of moral virtue and art. ... Therefore the true king is the same as the philosopher-legislator. As to the idea of imam in the Arabic language, it only signifies the one whose example is followed and who is well received. ... Only when all other arts, virtues, and activities seek to realize his purpose and no other, will his art be the most powerful art, his virtue the most powerful virtue, his deliberation the most powerful deliberation, and his science the most powerful science. ... So let it be clear to you that the idea of the philosopher, supreme ruler, king, legislator and imam is but a single idea.[5]

There are many more such examples and al-Fārābī's general theory of the philosopher-legislator fits both Shī'ī notions and, most specifically, those of al-Kirmānī which seem, in part, to have come from al-Fārābī's writings, either directly or through a process of interpretation. It is almost so obvious in this case that it seems appropriate to wonder about al-Fārābī's own religious affiliation. Can he have been a Shī'ī? And could, therefore, the theories of this kind that are found in his writings be credited to a Shī'ī source – one also used by al-Kirmānī? That is unlikely and a more complete review of what al-Fārābī actual says yields no support for regarding him as particularly oriented toward Shī'ism. His writings are devoid of religious doctrine or sympathy; he was not a theologian and did not advocate a religious teaching. When he employs the term imam, it has a general meaning only and cannot be taken in a technical Shī'ī sense. Still, the critical point is not whether al-Fārābī had actually proposed a philosophical interpretation of the imamate but whether others might easily elaborate such a theory on the basis of what he had said. Certainly, his theoretical understanding of the philosopher-imam lends itself readily to a re-interpretation like that given by al-Kirmānī wherein the legislator is the prophet and the imam is the interpreter, guardian and perpetuator of his law.

The next critical figure in the development of philosophy in Islam is Ibn Sīnā who, like al-Kirmānī, could easily be mistaken for a disciple of al-Fārābī, since their views and approaches are exceedingly similar. Ibn Sīnā, who lived from about 370/980 to 428/1037 was, moreover, a contemporary of al-Kirmānī, perhaps even precisely so since we know with certainty only the active period of al-Kirmānī's writings which run from 399/1008 to 411/1020. Understanding the connection between the two, especially in how each changed, elaborated or recast the ideas of al-Fārābī, would have its own intrinsic importance. Again De Smet offers some useful notes on aspects of this problem in his study of al-Kirmānī but, as with al-Fārābī, this remains a prime area for further research.

Could al-Kirmānī have known about Ibn Sīnā or vice versa? It is not at all impossible. The main difficulty is that Ibn Sīnā spent his whole career in Khurasan, where he was born, or in the Iranian cities of Gurjānj, Jurjān, Rayy, Iṣfahān and Hamadān, whereas we believe al-Kirmānī was active in Baghdad and then, for a short period, in Cairo. Both did live under, and in the case of Ibn Sīnā, work for Buyid rulers, though not the same ones.[6] Aside from a similar philosophical inclination, what makes the situation of Ibn Sīnā especially intriguing is that he admits himself in his autobiography that his own father and brother were Ismailis. Here is, under the circumstances, possibly an admission of the greatest importance. Accordingly, it is useful to quote him verbatim:

> My father was one of those who responded positively to the *dāʿī* of the Egyptians (i.e. the Fatimids) and he was reckoned to be one of the Ismailis. He had learned from them the account of the soul and intellect in the manner that they would speak about it and understand it. And likewise with my brother. Sometimes they used to discuss this among themselves while I was listening to them and comprehending what they were saying. I did not myself accept it, even though they began to appeal to me to do so.[7]

Thus we learn that the great philosopher came from an Ismaili family living in Khurasan in the period about 370/980 to 389/999. Who would have been the *dāʿī* he mentions? An answer to that question is quite difficult but his additional comment about a special Ismaili way of speaking about soul and intellect can only, under these conditions and its time and place, refer to doctrines taught by al-Sijistānī. He was the most prominent exponent of the Neoplatonic approach to soul and intellect, and we know that the *daʿwa* then advocated a position either based specifically on his writings or a version of it by someone else but following his lead. It is unlikely that Ibn Sīnā would mention an Ismaili doctrine of soul and intellect if it were not a matter that was specific to them. His comment can only point to the Neoplatonism of al-Sijistānī, even if it does not imply personal involvement by al-Sijistānī himself.[8]

But it is also interesting to ask here exactly what did Ibn Sīnā reject? Did he really refuse to become an Ismaili or was it necessary merely to state that in a public autobiography for purposes of *taqiyya* (dissimulation) and outward self-protection? Or, as yet another option, does he possibly mean that he could not accept the account of soul and intellect as taught by the *dāʿī*? Like al-Kirmānī, and in a similar way, Ibn Sīnā abandoned Neoplatonism in favour of an Aristotelian approach to philosophy in which the older concept of universal soul, for example, largely disappeared. His notion of intellect is equally at odds with that of al-Sijistānī and the Neoplatonists like him. In this regard his attitude was remarkably like that of al-Fārābī, as well as of al-Kirmānī.

As with al-Fārābī, however, this is not the place to lay out all the matters shared by Ibn Sīnā and al-Kirmānī except to note that there are many and that no one has yet undertaken the research necessary to identify and explain more than a few. Ibn Sīnā wrote a great deal more than al-Fārābī and his writings cover the issues in detail in instances where those of al-Fārābī are relatively brief. The task in his case is thus more formidable. Among his major philosophical treatises, however, there is one small piece that presents the whole scheme in the form of a mythic allegory. That is his version of the tale of Ḥayy ibn Yaqẓān which, unlike the better known account by Ibn Tufayl, makes of Ḥayy something like the master teacher, a kind of angelic agent intellect, or perhaps a prophet or an imam. Thus, in this version of the tale, the theme of teaching and being taught is central, whereas the Ḥayy of Ibn Tufayl is, by contrast, a self-taught autodidact. Because it has been wonderfully translated and explained by Henry Corbin in his *Avicenne et le récit visionnaire* (English translation *Avicenna and the Visionary Recital*),[9] this important work by Ibn Sīnā is readily available for interpretation in the present context. Perhaps its author never intended that it function as the allegory behind al-Kirmānī's *Rāḥat al-ʿaql* or the latter's great city of God, but there is enough correspondence to make such a suggestion not only interesting but likely to bear fruit.

Appendix B

Al-Kirmānī's Citations of His Own Works

Chapter Two included a complete survey of the titles attributed to al-Kirmānī in all the known sources, particularly of course, in his own writings and in the list provided by Idrīs 'Imād al-Dīn. It also contains an analysis of the order in which they were written based on the internal citations of one to another and the form, content, circumstances of composition, date or other information that helps make such a judgement feasible. A major difficulty in establishing the chronology of al-Kirmānī's works arises from the number of cross-references in them in which two books or treatises will cite each other. This tendency is most pronounced and inexplicable in the case of his *Rāḥat al-'aql* which mentions at least fifteen other titles and yet is cited itself in at least eight of these. However, as noted in Chapter Two, once it is removed from consideration by assuming that it was composed originally at a relatively earlier date and then revised in 411/1020, at the end of his active career, the remaining citations, with a few exceptions, provide useful indications of their probable chronological order. The purpose of this Appendix is simply then to offer as complete a list of the internal citations in al-Kirmānī's works as possible to support the conclusions reached in Chapter Two about the chronology and authenticity of these titles.

For the edition of a particular text or the manuscript used, see the Bibliography. For the manuscripts, which are cited here either by folio or page numbers depending on the manuscript, and which may not be accessible to others, the notations given below must serve merely to indicate the occurrences of a reference and not necessarily where to find it.

I: Extant Works

al-Risāla al-durriyya fī maʿnā al-tawḥīd wa'l-muwaḥḥid wa'l-muwaḥḥad
Cited in: *al-Muḍī'a, 44; al-Rawḍa, 81; al-Nuẓum,* 27
Cites: *Rāḥat al-ʿaql,* 22, 24
Known to Idrīs and al-Majdūʿ; known to Abū Muḥammad (a Yemeni Sunnī heresiographer of the 12th century)

Risālat al-nuẓum fī muqābalat al-ʿawālim baʿḍuhā baʿḍan bimā fīhā min al-mawjūdāt
Cites: *al-Durriyya,* 27; *al-Muḍī'a,* 28: *al-Waḍī'a,* 32
Known to Idrīs and al-Majdūʿ; known to Abū Muḥammad

al-Risāla al-Raḍiyya fī jawāb man yaqūl bi-qidam al-jawhar wa ḥudūth al-ṣūra
Cites: *al-Waḍī'a,* 36; *al-Waḥīda,* 40; *al-Muḍī'a,* 41

al-Risāla al-muḍī'a fī al-amr wa'l-āmir wa'l-ma'mūr wa fīhā radd min qawl ṣāḥib al-maqālīd
Cited in: *al-Nuẓum,* 28; *al-Raḍiyya,* 41; *Rāḥat al-ʿaql,* 22, 365; *al-Waḍī'a,* 16a, 51a; *al-Riyāḍ,* 63, 81, 126
Cites: a*l-Durriyya,* 44; *al-Rawḍa,* 45; *Rāḥat al-ʿaql,* 46, 52; *al-Waḍī'a,* 48; *al-Maṣābīḥ,* 53

al-Risāla al-lāzima fī ṣawm shahr Ramaḍān
Cites: *al-Ḥāwiya,* 78

al-Risāla al-rawḍa fi'l-azalī wa'l-azaliyya
Cited in: *al-Waḍī'a,* 16a; *al-Riyāḍ,* 81, 99, 218; *Rāḥat al-ʿaql,* 22–3, 60; *al-Zāhira,* 94; *al-Muḍī'a,* 45
Cites: *Mabāsim,* 90; *al-Zāhira,* 84; *al-Durriyya,* 81; *Rāḥat al-ʿaql,* 88
Known to Abū Muḥammad

al-Risāla al-zāhira fī jawāb masā'il
Citied in: *al-Rawḍa*, 84
Cites: *al-Rawḍa*, 94; *Rāḥat al-'aql*, 95

al-Risāla al-ḥāwiya fī'l-layl wa'l-nahār
Cited in: *al-Lāzima*, 78

Risālat mabāsim al-bishārāt bi'l-imām al-Ḥākim bi-Amr Allāh
Cited in: *Tanbīh*, 232, 234; *al-Rawḍa*, 90; *al-Wā'iẓa*, 142; *al-Kāfiya*, 151; *Rāḥat al-'aql*, 20
Cites: *al-Maṣābīḥ*, 118; *al-Kāfiya*, 118; *al-Shi'rī*, 130; *al-Waḥīda*, 131

al-Risāla al-wā'iẓa 'an masā'il al-māriq min al-dīn Ḥasan al-Farghānī
Cited in: *Tanbīh*, 207; *Rāḥat al-'aql*, 43, 124
Cites: *Mabāsim*, 142

al-Risāla al-kāfiya fī'l-radd 'alā al-Hārūnī al-Ḥusaynī al-Zaydī
Cited in: *Mabāsim*, 118; *Rāḥat al-'aql*, 20; *al-Waḍī'a*, 47b, 53a; *Tanbīh*, 203, 232
Cites: *al-Maṣābīḥ*, 151; *Tanbīh*, 165, 168

al-Maṣābīḥ fī ithbāt al-imāma
Cited in: *Mabāsim*, 118; *al-Kāfiya*, 151, *al-Aqwāl*, 94; *al-Muḍī'a*, 53; *Tanbīh*, 228, 232; *al-Waḍī'a*, 20b, 47b; *al-Riyāḍ*, 138, 190; *Rāḥat al-'aql*, 20, 22–3, 300, 359; *Ma'āṣim*, 45b
Cites: *Rāḥat al-'aql*, 155
Known to Idrīs and to al-Majdū' (pp. 121–3)

al-Aqwāl al-dhahabiyya
Cited in: *Ma'āṣim*, 2a, 2b, 25b, 64b, 70a, 76a, 101a
Cites: *Iklīl*, 2, 91, 97, 133: *al-Mafāwiz*, 101, 130; *al-Ḥadā'iq*, 97; *Tāj*, 97; *Rāḥat al-'aql*, 94, 97; *Maṣābīḥ*, 94; *al-Naqd*, 95; *Muqāyis*, 2; *al-Waḥīda*, 2
Known to Idrīs and to al-Majdū' (pp. 176–9)

al-Waḍī'a fī ma'ālim al-dīn wa uṣūlihā

Cited in: *al-Nuẓum,* 32; *al-Raḍiyya,* 36; *al-Muḍī'a,* 48; *Rāḥat al-'aql,* 22, 208, 265, 313, 333, 342, 353, 360; *al-Riyāḍ,* 138
Cites: *al-Waḥīda,* 14b, 29a, 41a, 43a, 47a, 103b; *Rāḥat al-'aql,* 15a, 26b, 47a; *al-Rawḍa,* 16a; *al-Muḍī'a,* 16a, 51a; *Tawḥīd,* 16b; *al-Maṣābīḥ,* 20b, 47b; *al-Kāfiya,* 47a, 53a
Known to Idrīs and to al-Majdū' (pp. 127–9)

Tanbīh al-hādī wa'l-mustahdī
Cited in: *Rāḥat al-'aql,* 16, 20, 22, 33, 395; *al-Kāfiya,* 165, 168
Cites: *al-Kāfiya,* 203, 232; *al-Wā'iẓa,* 207; *al-Maṣābīḥ,* 228, 232; *Mabāsim,* 232, 234
Known to Idrīs and to al-Majdū' (pp. 48–9)

Ma'āṣim al-hudā wa'l-iṣāba fī tafḍīl 'Alī 'alā al-ṣaḥāba
Cites: *al-Aqwāl,* 2a, 2b, 25b, 64b, 70a, 76a, 101a; *al-Maṣābīḥ,* 45b; *al-Ḥadā'iq,* 27b
Known to Idrīs only for the second part and likewise to al-Majdū' (pp. 95–6)

al-Riyāḍ
Cited in: *Rāḥat al-'aql,* 23, 364, 433
Cites: *al-Rawḍa,* 81, 99, 218; *al-Maṣābīḥ,* 138, 190; *Rāḥat al-'aql,* 59, 63, 79, 89, 93, 106, 107, 114, 125, 137, 151, 152, 160, 167; *al-Waḍī'a,* 138; *al-Muḍī'a,* 63, 81, 126; *al-Waḥīda,* 123, 126; *Ta'wīliyya,* 108; *al-Baṣriyya wa'l-Baghdādiyya,* 108
Known to Idrīs and to al-Majdū' (pp. 254–7)

Rāḥat al-'aql
Cited in: *al-Waḍī'a,* 15a, 26b, 47a; *al-Riyāḍ,* 59, 63, 79, 89, 93, 99, 106, 107, 114, 125, 137, 151, 152, 160, 167; *al-Zāhira,* 95; *al-Rawḍa,* 88; *al-Muḍī'a,* 46, 52; *al-Durriyya,* 22, 24; *al-Aqwāl,* 94, 97; *al-Maṣābīḥ,* 155
Cites: *Tanbīh,* 16, 20, 22, 33, 395; *al-Maṣābīḥ,* 20, 22–3, 300, 359; *Mabāsim,* 20; *al-Kāfiya,* 20; *al-Fihrist,* 25, 192; *al-Waḍī'a,* 22, 208, 265, 313, 333, 342, 353, 360; *al-Riyāḍ,* 23, 364, 433; *al-Muḍī'a,* 22–3, 365; *al-Rawḍa,* 22–3, 60; *al-Waḥīda,* 23, 25, 124, 361, 364, 383; *al-Wā'iẓa,* 43, 124; *al-Layliyya,* 123; (*al-*

Ḥāwiya?); *Tāj*, 313, 319, 421, 436; *Mīdān al-'aql*, 364, 433; *Muqāyis*, 364
Known to Idrīs and to al-Majdū' (pp. 280–4, but not seen by him?)

II: Lost Works

al-Shi'rī fi'l-khawāṣṣ
Cited in: *Mabāsim*, 130.

al-Muqāyis (*al-Maqāyis*)
Cited in: *Rāḥat al-'aql*, 364; *al-Aqwāl*, 2 (must have been written prior to *al-Aqwāl*)
Not found in the Yemen

al-Risāla al-layliyya
Cited in: *Rāḥat al-'aql*, 123 ('risālatnā al-ma'rūfa bi'l-layliyya' = *al-Ḥāwiya*?)

Risālat al-fihrist
Cited in: *Rāḥat al-'aql*, 20, 22–3, 25, 192
Not found in the Yemen

al-Waḥīda fi'l-ma'ād
Cited in: *Mabāsim*, 131; *al-Aqwāl*, 2; *al-Raḍiyya*, 40; *al-Waḍī'a*, 14b, 29a, 41a,, 43a (*Ma'ād*) 47a, 103b; *al-Riyāḍ*, 123, 126(*Ma'ād*); *Rāḥat al-'aql*, 23, 25, 124, 361, 364, 383 (must have been written prior to *al-Aqwāl*)
Must be the same as the *Fi'l-ma'ād* mentioned by Idrīs but not found in the Yemen. Cited by al-Kirmānī himself variously as either *al-Waḥīda* or *Fi'l-ma'ād* or both.

Tāj al-'uqūl
Cited in: *Rāḥat al-'aql*, 313, 319, 421, 436; *al-Aqwāl*, 97
Not found in the Yemen

Iklīl al-nafs wa tājuhā
Cited in: *al-Aqwāl,* 2, 91, 97, 133 (must have been written prior to *al-Aqwāl*)
Not found in the Yemen

Maydān al-ʿaql
Perhaps the *Kitāb maydān al-ʿuqūl* mentioned by Idrīs but not available in the Yemen
Cited in: *Rāḥat al-ʿaql,* 364, 433

al-Naqd wa'l-ilzām
Cited in: *al-Aqwāl,* 95
Not found in the Yemen

al-Mafāwiz
Perhaps *Risālat al-mafāwiz wa'l-ḥadā'iq,* mentioned by Idrīs but not available in the Yemen
Cited in: *al-Aqwāl,* 101, 130

al-Ḥadā'iq
Perhaps the same as the *Risālat al-mafāwiz wa'l-ḥadā'iq,* mentioned by Idrīs but not available in the Yemen (see also *al-Mafāwiz*)
Cited in: *Maʿāsim,* 27b; *al-Aqwāl,* 97

al-Risāla al-Ta'wīliyya
Cited in: *al-Riyāḍ,* 108
Not found in the Yemen

al-Majālis al-Baṣriyya wa'l-Baghdādiyya
Cited in: *al-Riyāḍ,* 108
Not found in the Yemen

al-Tawḥīd
Cited in: *al-Waḍī'a,* 16b (this is likely to be the same as *al-Durriyya*)

Appendix C

The Author's Table of Contents for the *Rāḥat al-ʻaql*

In Chapter Six we looked rather briefly at the structure of the *Rāḥat al-ʻaql* and could, under the circumstances there, hardly begin to examine much of its rich and exceedingly complex detail. Also, because al-Kirmānī employs in this work the technique of *mīzān al-diyāna* ('balance of religion') in such a way to almost obscure the very information a modern researcher might hope to glean from it, the book defies easy access and ready comprehension. His doctrines about the cosmic system, for example, occur in it piecemeal and in correspondence with purely religious matters – what he calls the *sunna al-ilāhiyya* (divine law). More than a few specific items needed to explain certain key points are either missing or unclear. Occasionally there appear also to be contradictions between a statement in one context and another. Nevertheless, the whole work is quite impressive, both in its scope and its content, and it surely belongs among the most interesting of all literary productions by the Ismaili *daʻwa.* Equally, despite the important work already done on it by De Smet in his *La Quiétude de l'intellect,* which constitutes itself an invaluable introduction to al-Kirmānī's many contributions, this book deserves a great deal of additional study by the scholars of Islamic science, philosophy and theology. But it is also necessary to admit that such investigations can and will prove frustrating for the reasons just stated. It is useful therefore to provide here an outline summary of it – in fact a translation of al-Kirmānī's own 'Table of Contents' – as an encouragement to further study by indicating what its author perceived as its overall theme and purpose and what he thought to include in it.

The following translation is based on the summary table of contents provided by al-Kirmānī both at the beginning of the *Rāḥat al-'aql* (pp.4–12) and at the commencement of each individual subsection of it. This version conforms to that given by the Egyptian editors for each subsection within the text. It matches the text of the one manuscript at my disposal but is slightly at odds with the wording in the table of contents at the beginning of the same edition. Ghālib's version, which seems to have been patched together from two differing manuscript sources, often has a reading that does not correspond precisely to this one.

Translation

This book is made up of seven ramparts and each rampart is comprised of seven pathways; the seventh rampart, however, includes fourteen pathways, since the seventh needed twice as many in order to complete the aim intended and the hope of attaining perfection in the next life. To finish it I seek the assistance of God and His friend on earth and I ask Him for infallibility and an inspiration for correctness, knowing that we ourselves are not free in this task from errors. And we have no power nor strength save through God, the Most High.

The First Rampart: The introduction to the book and an explanation of what understanding it requires of the reader, and the cause for the arrangement of the ramparts and its pathways as they have been arranged here. It comprises seven pathways.

The First Pathway: Concerning what is required to exhort the soul and prepare it to be receptive, and what will exhort it and prepare it prior to the reading of this book.

The Second Pathway: On what learning is required to begin with in order to read religious books and follow teachers and learn from this book of ours.

The Third Pathway: On what books must be read prior to this book and on making it the focus by assiduously considering what it contains.

The Fourth Pathway: On the purpose in arranging the ramparts of the book in the way we grouped them together with their pathways.

The Fifth Pathway: On the propitiousness accorded the person who reads this book in accord with the way of the faith of those who serve God, the exalted, through the monotheistic community, and the arrangement ordained in the rites of worship leading to salvation and blessedness in the abode of eternity and permanence.

The Sixth Pathway: On the tidings of he who reads this book not in accord with the faith and not following the arrangement of worship, such as those who do not display good works and who, by causing it to endure an eternal painful punishment, fall short of fully supporting the soul.

The Seventh Pathway: On what will accrue to the soul by reading this book and by comprehending what is in it and perceiving that it is beneficial for obtaining perfection.

The Second Rampart: On the affirming of God's absolute oneness, which is the crown of the intellects, and in sanctifying, praising and glorifying Him. It is comprised of seven pathways.

The First Pathway: On the God beside whom there is no god but He, and the falsity of His being a non-existent.

The Second Pathway: On the falsity of His being an existent.

The Third Pathway: That no attribute attains Him and He is not a body nor in body nor apprehensible by intellect or sensation.

The Fourth Pathway: That He is not form or matter and nothing is with Him, in His being He which performs the function of a matter in which He acts.

The Fifth Pathway: That He has no opposite or likeness.

The Sixth Pathway: That there is no language that can express Him in a way appropriate to Him.

The Seventh Pathway: That the most truthful statement of His absolute oneness, glory and affirmation is that which is of the kind that denies of Him the attributes that exist in created beings.

The Third Rampart: On the Pen which is the first existent being. It comprises seven pathways.

The First Pathway: On affirming the innovated being which is the first existent being and that its existence is not from its own essence, and that it is the cause to which the existent beings lead; and it is not body, nor a faculty in body, and it is external to the world of body.

The Second Pathway: On its existence being from the Most High, may He be sanctified, not by way of emanation, as the Philosophers maintain, but by way of innovation, and that seeking to comprehend the manner of its coming to exist is impossible.

The Third Pathway: On its being the innovation in itself and the innovated, the oneness, and the one in itself, and that it is the first existent being which nothing comes before and which no other than it precedes it in having existence.

The Fourth Pathway: On its being complete and eternal and that it does not change from how it is; and that it is one, having no likeness; and that it intellects only its own essence.

The Fifth Pathway: On the quiddity of its substance and what it is that is necessarily attached to it as attributes; and what it is that it must bear because of what its essence comprises; and what it is that is borne by it; and that it is one in some respect and multiple in others.

The Sixth Pathway: That its glory, splendour, beauty and delight with its own essence is too great to be described; and that it is forbidden to grasp what is external to it and from which it has its existence; and yet it yearns to do that even while being confused by it; and it is the greatest name and the greatest thing named.

The Seventh Pathway: On its being the first mover for all moveable objects, no matter in what way they move; and that it is the cause in the existence of what is other than it; and that in acting it has no need for anything other than its essence; and that it is intellect, the intellecting and the thing intellected.

The Fourth Rampart: On what exists on account of the innovation, which is the first innovated being, by means of procession, consisting of the Pen and the Tablet and the sublime principles which are the heavenly letters. It comprises seven pathways.

The First Pathway: On the manner of procession.

The Second Pathway: On the first processive being which is the second intellect and is called in the divine law the Pen;[1] and proving that it is a second existent being; and that in perfection it is like the first; and that it is body and not in a body; and that its existence was not the result of a primary intention.

The Third Pathway: On the second procession which is the first having the potentiality that is prime matter and which is called the Tablet; and that its existence comes from the first innovated being but not by first intention; and that it does not resemble the first, nor does it share with it what is characteristic of being the first procession; and what is the reason for that, and that it is the principle of the world of body; and that, with respect to innovated beings, it functions as does three among the numbers.

The Fourth Pathway: On the cause on account of which the existence of what exists from the first innovated being, which is the first existent being, is not of the same kind.

The Fifth Pathway: On the celestial letters which are the noble principles within the world of the first procession; and their number and what exists because of each of them and what is the manner of its existence.

The Sixth Pathway: On the cause on the basis of which it is necessary for the celestial letters to exist as seven intellects distinct from bodies; and their coming into existence on account of procession.

The Seventh Pathway: That the existent beings which exist because of the innovating, which is the first innovated being, by procession, have their existence without time; and that each of them is pure form except for prime matter; and that they are one in a certain respect and many in another; and that they intellect nothing but their own essences and what precedes them in existing; and that their form which is a form the human does not go beyond, infuses their radiance in bodies and souls as the active agent in them, and through them it is attached to the existence of existing beings.

The Fifth Rampart: On what exists because of the noble principles, which are the celestial letters. It consists of nature and the heavenly bodies. It comprises seven pathways.

The First Pathway: On the quiddity of nature and that it is a single thing in its essence in the world of body in respect to its substance and it is many things with respect to its actions in its materials.

The Second Pathway: That nature has two ends: the first end encompasses what it is caused to be in its initial existence and which constitutes its first perfection, and the second is encompassed by what it is caused to become upon a second existence and which constitutes its second perfection; and that its place is between these two ends, and what are these two ends, and what is the place of each, and that the second end is the centre around which motions move.

The Third Pathway: That nature has knowledge and of what is that knowledge; and that it is a combination of the virtues forming the reward that is its second end; and that it has self-sufficiency and completeness in that some portion of it is connected with others.

The Fourth Pathway: On the Footstool which is the near angel that is the first moving mover; and in what way it is a mover and which way it is the moving form for that in virtue of which it is called the sphere; and the reason for its being both mover and moved, and that it is inside the body and the reason for its being inside the body.

The Fifth Pathway: On the Throne which is the near angel that is the first moving mover for what moves and which is the moving body of that on account of which it is called the farthest sphere; and what follows it of the heavenly bodies and their number, and that the spheres in regard to what is in them are motionless in toto but moving in their individual parts.

The Sixth Pathway: On the bodies of the spheres and particularly that of the farthest sphere, and that they are the subtlest of bodies in the realm of nature, and that they accommodate no other form than the one they have.

The Seventh Pathway: On the states of the heavenly bodies and what functions to order for them to move as they do, and what are their divisions and actions which are the causes of the existence of the natural beings.

The Sixth Rampart: On what exists because of the heavenly bodies which are the mundane bodies and the various states they have. It comprises seven pathways.

The First Pathway: On the material on the basis of which there are bodies.

The Second Pathway: On the four qualities and their various states and the active form of nature, and in what manner some of them connect to others, and the difference between them and the heavenly bodies.

The Third Pathway: On the motions of the four qualities and that they have no gravity at their centre, nor colour, and that they are the medium through which souls perceive sensations.

The Fourth Pathway: That the four qualities are in their essences eternally durable and in their quantity invariable, without increase or diminution, and that they are at their limits transmutable into one another.

The Fifth Pathway: On the cause that necessitates the heaviness of bodies and the multiplicity of their parts.

The Sixth Pathway: That the earth is not circular and what is its cause and what way is it correctly the centre of the surrounding body, and what is its shape; and that the parts exposed to the air have a motion by which the water of the seas is transported and what is that motion, and that because of it lofty mountains were set in place and the cause for that.

The Seventh Pathway: That water does not envelop the surface of the earth and why that is, and that it increases and decreases in the oceans and why is that; and that the form appearing from it toward the air is the human form.

The Seventh Rampart: On what exists because of the heavenly and mundane bodies which make up the kingdoms and the various states of the human being in his perfection. It comprises fourteen pathways.

The First Pathway: On the second material out of which comes the generated beings in accord with the variations in mixture.

The Second Pathway: On the beings in the domain of air which accord with the effects mixed with it and their various states.

The Third Pathway: On the beings on the earth which consist of the minerals, plants and animals, but firstly in the minerals in so far as it is body.

The Fourth Pathway: On the mineral in so far as it is a natural soul and is possessed of actions and knowledge, and what are those actions and what is that knowledge.

The Fifth Pathway: On the plant in so far as it is body and that it is of a more complex composition and a more useful instrument than the minerals.

The Sixth Pathway: On the plant in so far as it is a growing soul and the manner of its existence, and its state with its body, and what is its quiddity.

The Seventh Pathway: On the animal in so far as it is body and the commencement of its appearance, and that it is more complex in composition than the plants and more useful an instrument, and that it is the end for beings beyond which there is no other being.

The Eighth Pathway: On the animal in so far as it is a sensing soul and its existence and the manner of its existence; and the existence of its understanding which is that by which it preserves its body; and what is its state in terms of its perfection and its power; and what is its origin and in what way does the species human agree and in what way does it differ.

The Ninth Pathway: On the soul of the human in so far as it senses and what is its state and what is it in itself, and what matters come into being in it and are consequent in existence to the first perfection it possesses by means of the acquisition of which it obtains the second perfection; and what is the end that it reaches in its actions; and what is that which has the function in it of matter and what has the function of form, and what is that which comes into being in it as the effect of acquisition, and what is its place in terms of the beings; and that it is one in some respects and many in another.

The Tenth Pathway: On the soul of the human in so far as it is rational and what is its state at this level; and is it the sensing soul itself operating at that level or does the human being have three souls, one vegetative, one sensing, and one rational, as some claim; and what is it, substance or accident? If it is substance, what bodies require in terms of accidents follows necessarily, or does it have accidents that are specific to it; and what is that which has the function in it of matter, and what is that of form.

The Eleventh Pathway: On the rational soul and what are its actions, and are these actions those that result from existing in cooperation and participation with its body, or does it have an action in which it stands apart from the body; and what is the difference between these actions, and what is the end it reaches in them; and what is its first perfection and what is its second, and what is the manner by which it becomes completely intellectual and eternal.

The Twelfth Pathway: On the rational soul in so far as it endures eternally and what is the cause of that, and what is that by which it earns eternity and ultimate happiness, and what is that by which it earns perdition and torment; and is that something it obtains from outside itself or in respect to its very nature on the basis of which has its existence; and what is the torment and what the happiness; and what is death, and what is its death and what is its life.

The Thirteenth Pathway: On the soul of humans, and what does it have after its transition in the way of reward in accord with its acquisition; and what is resurrection, what is the judgement, what is the recompense and what is the punishment, what is paradise and what is hellfire, and how is the state of the whole; and what is the state of the pious upon their return, and what is that which indicates in their worldly affairs what their state will be in the next life, and what are the actions of these people; and what is the state of the hypocrites and reprobates and those who lead astray and are led astray, and those who appoint themselves to the leadership among the ones who do not adhere to the true religion of God as they ought, and who are these people and what are their acts and what will await them after death; and do the souls attain their reward and punishment in the state of their transition or is it that they will all be together until the Day of Resurrection, and when will that be; and what brings together the two parties, the people of paradise and of hellfire, in order to make that clear; and is it a form distinct from what now is the form of their bodies in this world or what manner does it have; and does the soul, after it separates and stands apart from its person, reattach to another body, as claimed by the proponents of exaggerations and metempsychosis, or does it not? Does it remember the matters in which it was formerly involved in this world or not? Does its comprehension of things cease or not? Is the one delivered over to the reward distinguished by having an action that affects others as is the case with the intellects outside or not and what is this action?

The Fourteenth Pathway: On the soul of the human in so far as it is rational and yet also inspired from the heavens; and the manner in which it is linked to the holy spirit; and the reason why not all souls in one era are inspired and what is the cause for that; and what is the revelation by means of which they are inspired and how is that; and in what way is it attached to the aroused souls, and is it attached to them in their state when they are at the level of sensation, or at the level of imagination, or at the level of rationality? And what are its divisions, and what is the miracle that is manifested on their behalf; and what is the difference between it and what might be observed in the operations performed by a conjurer, and for what reason are those who are associated with conjurers possible to comprehend and understand, and those associated with the prophetic miracle not possible to comprehend or explain even by making an effort; and what excellences are brought together in the inspired soul and what is its state in terms of its actions and its aims in terms of its goals; and how is its power with respect to its associates and what are their ranks, and what is the rank of those appointed for the preservation of the community in their place, and what is he made to convey from God, the exalted; and how many are the ages and their associates through whom He completes the new creation; and what is the rank of the master of the seventh era and what are his actions, and how will one know of the completion of the eras; and a statement in refutation of the belief of the Philosophers in books of theirs regarding the achievement of the virtuous soul and exactly how it is wrong. But the ultimate reckoning is God's; how excellent a caretaker is He.

Notes

Chapter One

1. There is a natural tendency in dealing with the era of al-Ḥākim of becoming overwhelmed by the extremely fascinating and complex details of his life and reign which, however, it is safe to say, defy simple comprehension and adequate explanation. Our purpose here, however, is much simpler and that is to suggest what role al-Kirmānī played in it. What follows thus has a fairly narrow focus in respect to al-Ḥākim and it concentrates for the most part on the crucial years near the end of the reign when al-Kirmānī actually served the *da'wa* in Egypt. Nevertheless, his expression of devotion to al-Ḥākim is a noteworthy feature of all his writings, even those from the preceding period.

2. Many modern accounts of al-Ḥākim's rule exist and several are listed in the bibliography. In part the comments that follow here are specifically about the functioning of the *da'wa* and depend on an earlier study of mine entitled 'The Ismaili Da'wa in the Reign of the Fatimid Caliph Al-Ḥākim,' *Journal of the American Research Center in Egypt*, 30 (1993), pp. 161–82, which may be consulted for the background and sources.

3. On Idrīs, consult the entries by I. K. Poonawala in his *Biobibliography*, pp. 169–75, and 'Idrīs b. al-Ḥasan,' *EI2, Supplement*, p. 407.

4. The chief *qāḍī* was responsible for the administration of justice, an office of great importance and power. He controlled the courts, pious endowments, and weights and measures, for example. His sphere of activity would thus not normally involve teaching or any of the duties associated with the *da'wa.*

5. *Majālis* is the plural of *majlis,* as in *majālis al-ḥikma,* the regular 'sessions of wisdom' for the teaching of Ismaili doctrine.

6. There is some, mostly inadequate, information in our sources about many of these cases but they are all in all too numerous to discuss here. Based on the data presented to us by our sources, it would be hazardous, moreover, to attempt to be more specific. What is clear is that the imam often did not approve of the way these men performed their public duties.

7. The Dār al-'Ilm, also known as the Dār al-Ḥikma, is not the same as the *majālis al-ḥikma.* The former was a public academy and its professors were mostly Sunnī. The latter was exclusively for Ismailis and was directed by the Ismaili *dā'īs.* On this see my article 'Fatimid Institutions of Learning,' *Journal of the American Research Center in Egypt,* 34 (1997), pp. 179–200, as well as Heinz Halm's *The Fatimids and their Traditions of Learning* (London, 1997), pp. 27–9, 44–9, 71–8.

8. *Al-Waḍī'a,* 76a–77a.

9. The *ashrāf* (singular *sharīf*) are members of the *ahl al-bayt,* or descendants of the Prophet through either al-Ḥasan or al-Ḥusayn, the sons of 'Alī. By the time of al-Kirmānī, they had long been organized in formal corporations in the major cities of Islam, including Cairo/Fustat which, like Baghdad, had its own 'head of the *ashrāf*' (*naqīb al-ashrāf*).

10. On Fakhr al-Mulk, see Ibn Khallikān, *Biographical Dictionary,* tr. W. MacGukin de Slane (Paris, 1842–71), vol. 3, pp. 279–280, and Ibn al-Athīr, *al-Kāmil,* index and vol. 9, p. 260 (his death and burial).

11. i.e., the *ahl al-bayt,* 'People of the House', a term which the Shī'a use in reference to the Prophet's family and his direct descendants, including the imams.

12. Qur'ān, *Sūrat al-mulk* 67: 5: 'And We adorned the lower heaven with lamps, and made them things to throw at satans.'

13. There were in fact two separate appointments of Muḥammad al-Ashraf to the vizierate, both, however, of extremely short dura-

tion. After the second, he was caught fleeing into Syria by Badr al-Jamālī and put to death in 466/1074; al-Maqrīzī, *Itti'āẓ*, vol. 2, pp. 271, 313, 333. Some lines of poetry by him were recorded by al-Tha'ālibī in his *Tatimmat al-yatīma.* See also A. H. Saleh, 'Ibn Khalaf', *EI2*, *Supplement*, p. 390.

14. *Mabāsim*, pp. 129–30.

15. Ibn al-Jawzī, *al-Muntaẓam*, vol. 7, p. 107; al-Maqrīzī, *Itti'āẓ al-ḥunafā'*, vol. 1, p. 261.

16. Ibn al-Jawzī, *al-Muntaẓam*, vol. 7, pp. 237–8.

17. Ibn al-Athīr, *al-Kāmil*, vol. 9, p. 223.

18. Al-Iṣṭakhrī was the *qāḍī* Abu'l-Ḥasan 'Alī b. Sa'īd who died in 404; see his obituary in Ibn al-Athīr, *al-Kāmil*, vol. 9, p. 246.

19. McDermott, *The Theology of Shaikh al-Mufīd*, p. 30, item number 30.

20. *Mabāsim*, ed. Ghālib, pp. 113–14.

21. For simplicity I will use hereafter the dual form of this Arabic word in its oblique case only, rather than both *al-'ibādatān* and *'ibādatayn.*

22. It was, of course, also a point used by opponents against the Philosophers as well as the Sufis both of which groups spoke about inner, intelligible or spiritual realities which have an importance above or superior to the outward, tangible, mundane and literal aspects of the law and religion.

23. It was once assumed that al-Kirmānī arrived in Egypt about 408 when he wrote the *Risāla al-wā'iẓa* addressed to al-Akhram. But, as J. van Ess has shown, it is possible to date the *Mabāsim* to an earlier period, perhaps as much as two and a half or three years before the *Wā'iẓa.* The difficulties surrounding the earlier closing of the *majālis* and the deposition of al-Fāriqī, moreover, do not appear to be linked to al-Darazī and al-Akhram. There may have been some connetion but none is obvious in our data. That is one reason why al-Kirmānī's own words are so important, although they are not themselves quite clear about what he observed when he first arrived. It is less than certain, for that matter, whether he came because he was summoned or whether he might have been forced to flee Iraq. It is worth noting again that we possess only his statements and nothing else. That he was called to Egypt seems the most likely interpretation, and that al-Darazī, al-Akhram and Ḥamza are three of the extremists he mentions in the *Mabāsim* is equally plausible. But the problems in 405 were more complex.

24. In the chapter on the imamate where al-Kirmānī offers a list of imams running from Ḥasan b. 'Alī b. Abī Ṭālib through Muḥammad b. Ismā'īl, followed by the three concealed imams, and the Fatimid imams to al-Ḥākim bi-Amr Allāh al-Manṣūr Abū 'Alī, Amīr al-Mu'minīn (adding here, '*salām Allāh 'alayhim*'). At this point the text continues by naming al-Ẓāhir li-I'zāz Dīn Allāh Abū Ma'add and al-Mustanṣir bi'llāh Ma'add Abū Tamīm, Amīr al-Mu'minīn, '*salām Allāh 'alayhi wa 'alayhim ajma'īn*'. The author then adds to this: 'Many imams will come after them until the conclusion of the perfecting (*tatammun al-tamām*). God, the exalted, is He who increases just as He promised in His glorious Book, revealed to His chosen prophet ... "And We have bestowed on you the seven oft-repeated [*sab'an min al-mathānī*] and the mighty Qur'ān (15:87)".' Al-Mustanṣir's reign commenced in 427/1036, quite a bit later than the date for the final version of al-Kirmānī's *Rāḥat al-'aql* which is 411/1021 and which is often considered the date of his death. Does this mean that he survived into this later period? Or does the discrepancy between the initial recognition of al-Ḥākim as 'Master of the time' and this passage which extends the imamate down to al-Mustanṣir indicate the work of an editor other than al-Kirmānī himself?

Chapter Two

1. See his *Kanz al-fawā'id* (Beirut, 1985).
2. A Yemeni writer of the mid-6th/12th century by the name of Abū Muḥammad composed a work called *Mukhtaṣar fī 'aqā'id al-thalāth wa'l-sab'īn firqa* which contains a lengthy section on the Ismailis and their literature. This man had seen and read several works by al-Kirmānī, but he is the first and perhaps the only outsider to have had access to them as far as we can tell.
3. One is by an unknown author and the other by a later writer Shahiyār b. al-Ḥasan, who was a *dā'ī* in the era of al-Mustanṣir.
4. One is misspelled. On p. 285, in place of *al-waḍiyya*, read *al-raḍiyya*.
5. The first *Kitāb al-'aqā'id wa lubāb al-fawā'id*, which Poonawala did not cite in his *Biobibliography* despite carefully reviewing the material from Idrīs, suggests that it was not given by the manuscript he consulted. This suggestion was communicated to me by Professor Poonawala himself. It looks suspiciously like a title belonging to 'Alī b. al-Walīd, the *Lubāb al-fawā'id wa ṣafwa al-'aqā'id*. The second is more

of a problem. Poonawala included it and it may quite well belong to Idrīs's text. Still it is not very plausible that it is by al-Kirmānī.

6. In the printed text, which derives in any case from an unpunctuated manuscript source, a comma must be added between *Kitāb maydān al-'uqūl* and *Fi'l-ma'ād,* to yield two titles, not one.

7. There are several references to other works said to be by al-Kirmānī which for various reasons cannot be authentically attributed to him. One (no. 35 in Poonawala's list) is the *Risālat usbū' dawr al-satr* published by Arif Tamir in his *Arba' rasā'il Ismā'īliyya* (Salamiya, 1952, pp. 61–6). For the argument against its connection to al-Kirmānī, see De Smet, *La Quiétude,* p. 8. Another (Poonawala, no. 33, taken from Ivanow) is nothing more than a line of description given by Idrīs for the *Riyāḍ* (p. 285). It is not a separate title. No. 31 on Poonawala's list is the *Kitāb al-khazā'in* mentioned by Idrīs but which is nevertheless quite doubtful. Two other citations (Poonawala, nos 24 and 27) might reflect separate titles of independent works but both may also be references to other known works by al-Kirmānī. No. 24, *Risālatunā fī ma'rifat al-ḥudūd wa'l-ma'ād* (*Rāḥat al-'aql,* p. 34) could be a generic reference and not specific. No. 27 *Risālatunā al-ma'rūfa bi'l-layliyya* (*Rāḥat al-'aql,* p. 123) may well refer to his *al-Ḥāwiya.* Two more, a *Kitāb* (*Risālat*) *al-ma'ārij* (Poonawala, no. 34, *Rāḥat al-'aql,* p. 81) and a *Risālat al-tawḥīd* (*al-Waḍī'a,* 16b), are not cited explicitly as his own works. Nevertheless, the second, that discusses which of the angels are *ibdā'ī* and which *inbi'āthī,* could also be an alternate title for his *al-Durriyya.* However, it is not mentioned in any list of al-Kirmānī's works.

8. Against this supposition, it is true that the *Aqwāl* cites the *Maṣabīḥ* which may put it earlier and thus before both the *Aqwāl* and the *Ma'āṣim.*

9. The two citations of the *Tanbīh al-hādī* in the *Kāfiya* (pp. 165 and 168) do not, in fact, make obvious sense. The connection between the two works, however, is clear from the reference to the *Kāfiya* in the *Tanbīh* (p. 203). There, he refers back to an earlier refutation of the Zaydīs, namely the *Kāfiya,* but the context of the two references in the *Kāfiya* explains nothing obvious. I strongly suspect the original text of the latter read differently and another work was actually meant by the author. If so, additional manuscript research may reveal it.

10. 'Zur Chronologie der Werke des Hamīdaddīn al-Kirmānī' in 'Biobibliographische Notizen zur islamischen Theologie', *Die Welt des*

Orients, 9 (1978), pp. 259–61.

11. The speaking-prophets are those that issue the law and scripture, whereas the founders are their immediate successors whose role is to establish (i.e. to lay the foundation of) the interpretation (*ta'wīl*) of that same law and scripture.

12. *Majmū'at rasā'il al-Kirmānī*, pp. 102–12.

13. *Al-Risāla al-lāzima, fī ṣawm shahr Ramaḍān wa ḥīnihā'.* Ghālib's edition (*Majmū'at rasā'il al-Kirmānī*, pp. 61–80) gives the title without the phrase '*wa ḥīnihā*' which, however, occurs at the appropriate place in the text (p. 61) as if it is a part of the title. In fact the method of determining the advent of Ramaḍān, i.e. when it begins exactly, is the subject of the treatise.

14. This title presents a major difficulty in whether to regard it as one or two separate works. It appears as one in the list of Idrīs, discussed previously, but it occurs as a *Kitāb al-ḥadā'iq* in the *Aqwāl* (p. 97) and the *Ma'āṣim* (27b) and as *Risālat al-mafāwiz* in the *Aqwāl* (pp. 101 and 130). Nevertheless, given that al-Kirmānī can be imprecise in the citations of his own treatises, I am inclined to regard this as a single work.

15. It is unclear whether this title should be read as *al-Muqāyis* (comparing) or *al-Maqāyis*, pl. of *al-miqyās* (measure).

16. It should be noted that the alternate form of this title *Mīzān al-'aql* in the printed versions of the *Rāḥat al-'aql* is not supported by the manuscript I consulted, which reads clearly *Maydān al-'aql* in both instances (pp. 364 and 433).

17. It mentions both the *Muqāyis* and the *Maydān al-'aql* in the same passage (p. 364).

18. Abū Ḥātim al-Rāzī, *A'lām al-nubuwwa*, ed. Ṣalāḥ al-Ṣāwī and Ghulāmriḍā A'wānī (Tehran, 1977).

19. Edited by P. Kraus in his *Rasā'il falsafiyya li-Abī Bakr Muḥammad b. Zakariyā al-Rāzī*, pp. 15–96; English trans. A. Arberry, *The Spiritual Physick.* This volume, assembled by Kraus in 1939, included also the Arabic text of a key passage from Abū Ḥātim's *A'lām al-nubuwwa* (pp. 291–316) which Kraus labelled 'al-Munāẓarāt bayn al-Rāzayn'. He likewise made use of the text of al-Kirmānī's *al-Aqwāl* in his edition of the *Ṭibb al-rūḥānī.*

20. See *al-Aqwāl*, p. 2.

21. There seems to be a number of manuscripts of this second part. I have examined two that are held by The Institute of Ismaili Studies in London. In one of them, 724, as an example, mention of

al-Jāḥiẓ or the *'Uthmāniyya* occurs at the following places: 99a, 101a, 101b, 109b, 111b, 112b, and 122a among others. On these Mss., see Gacek, *Catalogue of Arabic Manuscripts in the Library of The Institute of Ismaili Studies* (London, 1984), vol. 1, p. 55.

22. *Ma'āṣim*, 108b.

23. Published by Ghālib in the*Majmū'at rasā'il al-Kirmānī*, pp. 148–82.

24. Published by Ghālib in the *Majmū'at rasā'il al-Kirmānī*, pp. 113–33, and previously by Ḥusayn in *Tā'ifat al-Durūz*, pp. 52–71; and Ghālib in his *al-Ḥaraka al-bāṭiniyya fi'l-Islām*, pp. 205–34.

25. Published by Ghālib in the *Majmū'at rasā'il al-Kirmānī*, pp. 19–26 and earlier by M. K. Ḥusayn (Cairo, 1952). The title as given by the author in the text is simply *al-Risāla al-durriyya* (Ghālib, p. 20) which is also given by the Tübingen Ms. I consulted.

26. Published by Ghālib in the *Majmū'at rasā'il al-Kirmānī*, pp. 27–34, and by M. K. Ḥusayn (Cairo, 1952). The word *nuẓum* (pl. of *niẓām*) in the title might be read *naẓm* (order, arrangement).

27. Ghālib in the *Majmū'at rasā'il al-Kirmānī*, pp. 35–42.

28. Ghālib in the *Majmū'at rasā'il al-Kirmānī*, pp. 43–60.

29. These comments do not serve to characterize the fully developed doctrine of the Druze in regard to al-Ḥākim but merely to suggest what al-Kirmānī thought about the pronouncements of al-Akhram and his associates at this early date. It seems clear from the *Wā'iẓa* that the situation was still fluid, although rapidly moving in a direction quite repugnant to the leaders of the *da'wa*. Al-Kirmānī may well have persisted in the faint hope that the dissidents would see the light and return to the fold.

30. We know a little about the violence that resulted from the preaching of al-Akhram, al-Darazī and Ḥamza, but there is no evidence for, or suggestion of, the direct involvement in it of the *da'wa*.

31. It is also badly printed. The 'edition' of A. Tamir (Beirut, 1960) is quite unreliable. In the case of this work also we have one manuscript which is truly old, even as early as the 6th/12th century. See François de Blois, 'The Oldest Known Fāṭimid Manuscript from Yemen', *Proceedings of the Seminar for Arabian Studies,* Offprint from Vol. 14 (1984), pp. 1–7.

32. Note particularly in this regard the comments of al-Majdū' (pp. 255–6), especially the lines of poetry from two Ṭayyibī authors he qoutes in praise of it.

33. *Rāḥat al-'aql*, p. 23.

34. For editions, see the bibliography. Note also the evaluation of these editions by De Smet in his *La Quiétude de l'intellect*, p. 9, n. 25.

Chapter Three

1. p. 51. I have collated the text of this passage from this Ms. with the corresponding portion of the Fyzee Ms. and made a few adjustments.
2. Such as the two cases cited in the *Mabāsim*, p. 125.
3. Examples: *al-Muḍī'a*, pp. 45 and 59.
4. *Rāhat al-'aql*, pp. 18–19.
5. *Tanbīh al-hādī*, pp. 43, 64, 67, 74, 81, 89; *Ma'āṣim*, 108b.
6. *Al-Maṣābīḥ*, pp. 145–6.
7. *Al-Waḍī'a*, 103b.
8. *Al-Riyāḍ*, p. 88.
9. *Al-Aqwāl*, p. 137.
10. *Rāḥat al-'aql*, pp. 285–6.
11. *Rāḥat al-'aql*, pp. 259–60. The *ḥujja* occupies the highest rank in the *da'wa* except that of the imam's *bāb*. There would be theoretically twelve *ḥujjas*, one to command each of the twelve regions (*jazīras*) of the inhabited world. For more on the ranks in the *da'wa* and the concept of hierarchy (*ḥudūd*), see Chapter Six.
12. *Al-Wā'iẓa*, p. 144.
13. *Rāḥat al-'aql*, pp. 18–19.
14. An example: *Rāḥat al-'aql*, pp. 191 and 192.
15. *Al-Riyāḍ*, pp. 173–4.
16. *Rāḥat al-'aql*, p. 437.
17. *Tanbīh al-hādī*, 15th *Bāb, Faṣls*, 1 and 2.
18. *Tanbīh al-hādī*, pp. 125–7.
19. *Tanbīh al-hādī*, p. 205.
20. *Tanbīh al-hādī*, pp. 127–35, 144, 147; *Rāḥat al-'aql*, p. 165.
21. *Tanbīh al-hādī*, pp. 149–53.
22. *Tanbīh al-hādī*, pp. 189–99.
23. Paul Kraus, 'Hebräische und syrische Zitate in ismā'īlitischen Schriften', *Der Islam*, 19 (1931), pp. 243–63; and A. Baumstark, 'Zu den Schriftzitaten al-Kirmānīs', *Der Islam*, 20 (1932), pp. 308–13.
24. *Al-Maṣābīḥ*, *al-Waḍī'a*, *Rāḥat al-'aql* and *Ma'āṣim.*
25. This man assumed the vizierate in 436 upon the death of al-Jarjarā'ī and he was killed in 440.
26. *Al-Kāfiya*, p. 159.

27. *Ma'āṣim,* 118a.
28. *Ma'āṣim,* 103b and elsewhere.
29. *Ma'āṣim,* 81b, 12b and elsewhere.
30. *Tanbīh al-hādī,* p. 177.
31. *Rāḥat al-'aql,* p. 363; there are many other references to this al-Rāzī which do not cite a book (other than his *al-Ṭibb al-rūḥānī,* already discussed).
32. *Al-Riyāḍ,* pp. 126, 128, 218.
33. *Al-Maṣābīḥ,* p. 125; *al-Waḍī'a,* 31a.
34. *Al-Kāfiya,* p. 165 and *Rāḥat al-'aql,* p. 22. On these works of al-Qāḍī al-Nu'mān, see in general the entry by I. K. Poonawala in his *Biobibliography,* pp. 48–68.
35. For the seven heavenly letters, see *al-Durriyya,* p. 25, where curiously he gives as the letters *f, r, d, i, a, l* and *m*; *Rāḥat al-'aql,* p. 34; and *al-Riyāḍ,* pp. 79, 105, 157, where he comments on the allusion to them by the masters in their statements about *kūnī-qadar.* For Jadd, Fatḥ and Khayāl, see *al-Waḍī'a,* 43a; *al-Riyāḍ,* pp. 165, 168 (Jadd); and *Rāḥat al-'aql,* pp. 409–16. For *al-sābiq, al-tālī,* the Pen and the Tablet, see *al-Waḍī'a,* 16b and 45a. It must be admitted that these citations are few indeed considering the previous importance in Ismaili thought of these ideas.
36. In addition to the smaller treatises which deal with elements in al-Sijistānī's teachings, the *Riyāḍ* (pp. 72–3, 91–3, 94, 220) mentions besides the *Nuṣra,* his *al-Iftikhār* and *al-Maqālīd.* The *Waḍī'a* (50a) also cites his *al-Iftikhār.*
37. See the comment he makes about them and this teaching in his autobiography, quoted here in Appendix A.
38. *Al-Riyāḍ,* pp. 213–14.

Chapter Four

1. Qur'ān 3: 7.
2. For more on what can be said about the *da'wa* during the reign of al-Ḥākim, see my study 'The Ismaili Da'wa in the reign of the Fatimid Caliph al-Ḥākim', *Journal of the American Research Center in Egypt,* 30 (1993), pp. 161–82, and the various primary and secondary works cited in it.
3. *Rāḥat al-'aql,* p. 256.
4. It is also true of many Sufis.
5. Al-Kirmānī also wrote a *al-Risāla al-muḍī'a,* thereby raising the

question of the relationship between the terms *muḍī'a* and *waḍī'a*, both of which appear to have the same root. Unfortunately, there are few if any other works with a title based on *wāḍī'a*, as such, and therefore al-Kirmānī's exact intention with this term, which he does not explain himself, is not certain.

6. See *Rāḥat al-'aql*, p. 385, where the same metaphor appears. Note that in early Ismaili doctrine 'Alī is not an imam but rather the Executor *(waṣī)*or Founder *(asās)*. This position is clearly above that of the imams who follow. In the writing of that time, the first imam is Ḥasan, his eldest son. However, al-Kirmānī also speaks of 'Alī as the first imam. I am, therefore, not quite sure of his position on this point.

7. *Al-Waḍī'a*, 8b.
8. *Al-Waḍī'a*, 9b–10a.
9. *Tanbīh al-hādī*, 30.
10. *Al-Maṣābīḥ*, p. 54.
11. *Al-Maṣābīḥ*, pp. 64–5.
12. *Al-Waḍī'a*, 10a–b.
13. *Al-Waḍī'a*, 10b.
14. *Tanbīh al-hādī*, p. 93.
15. *Al-Aqwāl*, pp. 114–15.
16. *Al-Kāfiya*, p. 152.
17. *Al-Riyāḍ*, p. 229.
18. *Al-Waḍī'a*, 11a.
19. *Al-Waḍī'a*, 40a.
20. *Al-Maṣābīḥ*, p. 61.
21. *Al-Waḍī'a*, 96b.
22. *Al-Waḍī'a*, 27b.
23. *Rāḥat al-'aql*, pp. 378–9.

Chapter Five

1. *Al-Waḍī'a*, 11a-b, specifically citing Qur'ān 50: 6–8; 88: 17–20; 20: 29; 86: 5–7; 51: 20; and 27: 84.
2. *Rāḥat al-'aql*, pp. 37–8.
3. *Al-Maṣābīḥ*, pp. 35–7.
4. *Al-Muḍī'a*, p. 47.
5. The means for apprehending something beyond the senses are these five techniques: *ḥadd* (definition), *qisma* (division), *taḥlīl* (analysis), *tarkīb* (composition) and *burhān* (demonstration). See

Ma'āṣim al-hudā, 48a; *Rāḥat al-'aql*, p. 44.

6. *Rāḥat al-'aql*, pp. 40–1.

7. *Rāḥat al-'aql*, pp. 51–3.

8. *Rāḥat al-'aql*, pp. 124, 126, 127–9.

9. On the use of this verb and its derivatives, see particularly *al-Riyāḍ*, p. 72.

10. *Rāḥat al-'aql*, pp. 75–9.

11. It is eternal once it has been brought into being.

12. *Rāḥat al-'aql*, pp. 89–94, 'huwa al-muḥarrik al-awwal al-ladhī lā yataḥarrik' and 'lā yuḥtāj fī'l-fi'l ilā ghayr dhātihi'.

13. *Rāḥat al-'aql*, p. 98.

14. *Al-Riyāḍ*, pp. 75–9. 'The second, which is called the soul, is not in motion'. But this situation is not completely clear as he also indicates that the outermost sphere does not move.

15. *Rāḥat al-'aql*, p. 196.

16. *Rāḥat al-'aql*, pp. 124, 129, 137.

17. In general and in addition to the citations given here in the notes, see the long and quite detailed study by De Smet of the content and problems in al-Kirmānī's doctrines regarding the ten intellects and the spheres. It forms chapter five '*Le Plérôme des dix intelligences*' (pp. 197–309, especially pp. 270–281, for the problems of the spheres) of his *La Quiétude de l'intellect*. One part of the problem stems from what appear to be two slightly different accounts which, I suspect, arise for al-Kirmānī because he is trying both to match the scheme proposed by al-Fārābī and at the same time to modify it. A major issue, for example, is whether or not the first intellect corresponds to a sphere or not. If it does not, as I have stated here, then the tenth must be that for the moon. However, although I trust what I have given is what al-Kirmānī intended, I admit the matter is not certain or without ambiguity, and there are possibly some contradictions in his statements.

18. On the tenth intellect as the 'active intellect' (*al-'aql al-fa' 'āl*), see *Rāḥat al-'aql*, pp. 127–9.

19. He also states that the first intellect is the Pen and the second is the Tablet, see *al-Waḍī'a*, 33a. But in the *Rāḥat al-'aql*, p. 101, he claims that first intellect is the Pen and yet also that second intellect is the Pen, whereas the second is in one place the Tablet and in the other also the Tablet. Perhaps, he means that the intellects are the pen(s), and the material entity that corresponds to them are all the tablet(s).

20. *Rāḥat al-'aql*, pp. 108–110.

21. On soul, see *al-Riyāḍ*, pp. 120–2.

22. The lower order beings derive their qualities from those higher so that they imitate or represent the higher order beings in their own lower realm, but the higher intellects are not universal abstractions or idealizations of lower beings.

23. *Al-Riyāḍ*, pp. 75–6.

24. *Rāḥat al-'aql*, p. 263.

25. He makes an interesting point out of the necessity for these minor elliptic motions in the greater orbits of the spheres. There are six for each of the seven and thus forty-two in all and this fact requires, in his view, six imams for each of the seven *nāṭiqs*; see *Rāḥat al-'aql*, p. 187.

26. 'lā li-ajlihi bal li-ajlihā,' *al-Aqwāl*, p. 90.

27. *Al-Maṣābīḥ*, p. 40, see also p. 30.

28. *Al-Aqwāl*, p. 28.

29. This is the principal theme of al-Kirmānī's *al-Aqwāl al-dhahabiyya* but it appears in many places, for example, *Rāḥat al-'aql*, p. 354.

30. *Al-Aqwāl*, pp. 89–90.

31. *Al-Aqwāl*, p. 73

32. *Al-Waḍī'a*, 14a–16b; *al-Riyāḍ*, p. 222.

33. *Rāḥat al-'aql*, pp. 124, 137, 145.

34. *Rāḥat al-'aql*, p. 146.

35. *Al-Waḍī'a*, 14a; *al-Raḍiyya*, p. 36.

Chapter Six

1. *Rāḥat al-'aql*, pp. 28–9.

2. *Al-Lāzima*, p. 76, for example; see De Smet, *La Quiétude*, p. 17.

3. See, for example, the use of this boat image in the *Rāḥat al-'aql*, p. 248.

4. *Rāḥat al-'aql*, p. 244.

5. *Al-Maṣābīḥ*, p. 75; also p. 62.

6. *Al-Riyāḍ*, p. 229.

7. *Ma'āṣim al-hudā*, 40b.

8. *Al-Aqwāl*, p. 91.

9. *Rāḥat al-'aql*, p. 169.

10. On the 'prophetic art', see *Rāḥat al-'aql*, p. 343.

11. *Rāḥat al-'aql*, p. 102.

12. *Al-Riyāḍ*, p. 89.
13. *Rāḥat al-'aql*, p. 186.
14. Ibid., pp. 375–6.
15. Ibid., pp. 409–10.
16. Ibid., p. 404.
17. Ibid., pp. 419–20. Daysān and Ibn al-Muqanna' are his examples of false prophets.
18. *Rāḥat al-'aql*, pp. 15–16.
19. Ibid., p. 191.
20. Ibid., p. 273.
21. *Al-Aqwāl*, pp. 28–9.
22. On the *waṣī/asās*, see *al-Riyāḍ*, pp. 83–5, 86, 90; *Rāḥat al-'aql*, p. 102 (where he states that the *waṣī* is the first imam).
23. *Al-Waḍī'a*, 29a.
24. *Tanbīh al-hādī*, p. 197.
25. *Rāḥat al-'aql*, p. 297.
26. *Al-Waḍī'a*, 39a.
27. *Rāḥat al-'aql*, pp. 208–10.
28. Ibid., pp. 134–8.
29. On this technique of exposition, see in addition to De Smet's comments in *La Quiétude de l'intellect*, his article '*Mīzān al-diyāna*'.
30. Assuming that he is describing the real state of affairs and not merely a theoretical model of what might exist under ideal conditions. Given the relatively extensive detail in his account for the lesser ranks of the *da'wa*, I suspect it actually was as he describes it, at least within the domain of the Fatimid caliphs where it could be implemented and maintained with some ease.
31. *Al-Waḍī'a*, 97a.
32. *Tanbīh al-hādī*, pp. 30, 53, 54.
33. *Al-Riyāḍ*, pp. 122–3.
34. *Rāḥat al-'aql*, p. 15. On the second perfection, see also *Rāḥat al-'aql*, pp. 33, 74, 83; *al-Riyāḍ*, pp. 59, 73, 79–80, 88.
35. *Al-Riyāḍ*, pp. 132–3.
36. Ibid., p. 75. See also, for example, *Rāḥat al-'aql*, p. 84.
37. He says an angel is 'pure form without matter,' i.e. the separate intellects as they exist without matter. See *al-Waḍī'a*, 14a; *al-Riyāḍ*, p. 222.
38. *Rāḥat al-'aql*, p. 434.

Appendix A

1. Al-Sijistānī, in contrast, barely discussed the imamate, either in theory or in actuality, and he does not name a reigning imam.

2. Arabic text edited with English translation by Richard Walzer (Oxford, 1985).

3. Arabic text edited by Fauzi M. Najjar (Beirut, 1964); partial English translation by him in *Medieval Political Philosophy: A Sourcebook*, ed. R. Lerner and M. Mahdi (Ithaca, NY, 1963), pp. 31–57.

4. English translation by M. Mahdi, *Alfarabi's Philosophy of Plato and Aristotle* (Ithaca, NY, 1969). Part of the same translation for the 'Attainment of Happiness' appears in *Medieval Political Philosophy*, pp. 58–82.

5. *Taḥṣīl al-saʿāda*, ed. Jaʿfar Āl Yāsīn (Beirut, 1983), pp. 92–3. The passage here is from the 'Attainment of Happiness' as trans. by Muhsin Mahdi in *Alfarabi's Philosophy of Plato and Aristotle*, pp. 46–7, with a few modifications.

6. On Ibn Sīnā in general, but specifically for his biography, see the article 'Avicenna' by various authors in the *Encyclopaedia Iranica*, vol. 3, pp. 66–110. The subentry on the biography is by Dimitri Gutas.

7. Arabic text and English translation by W. E. Gohlman, *The Life of Ibn Sina* (Albany, NY, 1974), pp. 18–19. I have modified Gohlman's translation slightly.

8. He was, by my reckoning, no longer alive, although others have tried to suggest that he could have lived until then.

9. English translation by Willard R. Trask (New York, 1960). The tale of Ḥayy appears on pp. 137–50.

Appendix C

1. There seems to be a contradiction here since he declared earlier in the title of the Third Rampart that the first existent being is the Pen. For a possible resolution, see note 19 in Chapter Five.

Bibliography

Abū Muḥammad, *Mukhtaṣar fī 'aqā'id al-thalāth wa'l-sab'īn firqa*. Ms. Istanbul 'Atif 1373; photocopy Indiana University Library.

al-Anṭākī, Yaḥyā b. Sa'īd, *History*, ed. 'Umar 'Abd al-Salām Tadmūrī, Ṭarābilis, Lubnān, 1990.

Assaad, Sadik A., *The Reign of al-Hakim bi Amr Allah (386/996–411/1021): A Poitical Study*, Beirut, 1974.

Baumstark, A., 'Zu den Schriftzitaten al-Kirmānīs,' *Der Islam*, 20 (1932), pp. 308–13.

Bosworth, C. Edmund, 'Bahā' al-Dawla', *EI2*, *Supplement*, pp. 118–19.

—— 'Mazyad, Banū,' *EI2*, vol. 6, pp. 965–6.

Bryer, David R., 'The Origins of the Druze Religion,' *Der Islam*, 52 (1975), pp. 47–84 and 239–64, and 53 (1976), pp. 5–27.

Corbin, Henry, *Avicenna and the Visionary Recital*, trans. by Willard R. Trask, New York, 1960.

Daftary, Farhad, *The Ismā'īlīs: Their History and Doctrines*, Cambridge, 1990.

De Smet, Daniel, 'Le *Kitâb Râḥat al-'Aql* de Ḥamîd al-Kirmânî et la cosmologie ismaélienne à l'époque fatimide,' *Acta Orientalia Belgica*, 7 (1992), pp. 81–91.

—— '*Mīzān ad-diyāna* ou l'équilibre entre science et religon dans la pensée ismaélienne,' *Acta Orientalia Belgica*, 8 (1993), pp. 247–

54.
—— 'Le Verbe-impératif dans le système cosmologique de l'ismaélisme,' *Revue des Sciences Philosophiques et Théologiques,* 73 (1987), pp. 397–412.
—— *La Quiétude de l'intellect: Néoplatonisme et gnose ismaélienne dans l'oeuvre de Ḥamîd ad-Dîn al-Kirmânî (Xe/XIe s.),* Louvain, 1995.
de Blois, François, 'The Oldest Known Fāṭimid Manuscript from Yemen,' *Proceedings of the Seminar for Arabian Studies,* Offprint from vol. 14 (1984), pp. 1–7.
al-Fārābī, Abū Naṣr, *Al-Farabi on the Perfect State: Abū Naṣr al-Fārābī's Mabādi' ārā' ahl al-madīna al-fāḍila,* ed. and trans. by Richard Walzer, Oxford, 1985.
—— *Alfarabi's Philosophy of Plato and Aristotle,* trans. by Muhsin Mahdi, Ithaca, NY, 1969.
—— *Kitāb al-siyāsa al-madaniyya,* ed. Fauzi M. Najjar, Beirut, 1964.
—— *Taḥṣīl al-sa'āda,* ed. Ja'far Al-Yāsīn, Beirut, 1983.
Gacek, Adam, *Catalogue of Arabic Manuscripts in the Library of The Institute of Ismaili Studies,* vol. 1, London, 1984.
Ghālib, Muṣṭafā, *al-Ḥaraka al-Baṭiniyya fi'l-Islām,* Beirut, 1982.
Goriawala, Mu'izz, *A Descriptive Catalogue of the Fyzee Collection of Ismaili Manuscripts,* Bombay, 1965.
Halm, Heinz, *The Fatimids and their Traditions of Learning,* London, 1997.
al-Hamdānī, Ḥusayn, *Maqālāt kitāb al-riyāḍ l'l-shaykh Aḥmad al-Kirmānī,* Hyderabad, 1358/1939.
Ḥusayn, Muḥammad Kāmil, *Ṭā'ifat al-durūz,* Cairo, 1962.
Ibn al-Athīr, 'Izz al-Dīn, *al-Kāmil fi'l-ta'rīkh,* ed. C. J. Tornberg, Leiden, 1964 (Beirut reprint).
Ibn al-Jawzī, 'Abd al-Raḥmān, *al-Muntaẓam,* vol. 7, Hyderabad, 1939.
Ibn Sīnā, Abū 'Alī, *The Life of Ibn Sina,* ed. and trans. by W. E. Gohlman, Albany, NY., 1974.
Idrīs, 'Imād al-Dīn b. al-Ḥasan, *'Uyūn al-akhbār,* vol. 6, ed. M. Ghālib, Beirut, 1984.
Ivanow, W., *Ismaili Literature: A Bibliographical Survey,* Tehran, 1963.
Jiwa, Shainool, 'Fāṭimid-Būyid Diplomacy During the Reign of al-'Azīz Billāh (365/975–386/996),' *Journal of Islamic Studies,* 3 (1992), pp. 57–71.
al-Karājikī, *Kanz al-fawā'id,* Beirut, 1985.
al-Kirmānī, Ḥamīd al-Dīn Aḥmad, *al-Risāla al-durriyya fī ma'nā al-tawḥīd,* ed. M. Kāmil Ḥusayn, Cairo, 1952; ed. M. Ghālib in

Majmū'at rasā'il al-Kirmānī, pp. 19–26. Ms. Tübingen University.

—— *al-Risāla al-lāzima*, ed. Muḥammad 'Abd al-Qādir 'Abd al-Nāṣir in *Majallat Kulliyyat al-Ādāb, Jāmi'at al-Qāhira*, 31 (1979), pp. 1–52; ed. M. Ghālib in *Majmū'at rasā'il*, pp. 61–80.

—— *Risālat al-nuẓum fī muqābalat al-'awālim*, ed. M. Kāmil Ḥusayn, Cairo, 1952 (with *al-Durriyya*); ed. M. Ghālib in *Majmū'at rasā'il*, pp. 27–34. Ms. Tübingen University.

—— *al-Risāla al-raḍiyya*, ed. M. Ghālib in *Majmū'at rasā'il*, pp. 35–42. Ms. Tübingen University.

—— *al-Risāla al-waḍī'a fī ma'ālim al-dīn*, Ms. Fyzee Collection, Bombay University Library.

—— *al-Risāla al-wā'iẓa*, ed. M. Kāmil Ḥusayn in *Majallat Kulliyyat al-Ādāb, Jāmi'a Fu'ād al-Awwal*, 14 (1952), pp. 1–29; ed. M. Ghālib in *Majmū'at rasā'il*, pp. 134–47.

—— *Kitāb al-maṣābīḥ fī ithbāt al-imāma*, ed. M. Ghālib, Beirut, 1969.

—— *Kitāb al-riyāḍ*, ed. 'Ārif Tāmir, Beirut, 1960; Ms. Hamdani Collection.

—— *Kitāb ma'āṣim al-hudā wa'l-iṣāba fī tafḍīl 'Alī 'alā al-ṣaḥāba*, Ms. 724, copied in Sūrat 1356/1937 and 107, undated, The Institute of Ismaili Studies Library, London. All specific citations, by folio number, are to Ms. 724.

—— *Kitāb rāḥat al-'aql*, ed. M. Kāmil Ḥusayn and M. M. Ḥilmī, Cairo, 1953; ed. M. Ghālib, Beirut, 1967; Ms. Hamdani Collection (from photocopy ARCE, Cairo).

—— *Kitāb tanbīh al-hādī wa'l-mustahdī*, Ms. 723, in The Institute of Ismaili Studies Library, London. (See Gacek, p. 152). Ms. Fyzee Collection, Bombay University Library, no. 57 (Goriawala). References by page number to the first of these.

—— *Majmū'at rasā'il al-Kirmānī*, ed. M. Ghālib, Beirut, 1983 (Containing *al-Durriyya, al-Nuẓum, al-Raḍiyya, al-Muḍī'a, al-Lāzima, al-Rawḍa, al-Zāhira, al-Ḥāwiya, Mabāsim, al-Wā'iẓa, al-Kāfiya*, and two treatises *Fī'l-radd 'alā man ankara [yunkiru] al-'ālam al-rūḥānī* and *Khazā'in al-adilla* not by al-Kirmānī).

—— *Risālat mabāsim al-bishārāt*, in Ḥusayn, *Ṭā'ifat al-durūz*, pp. 52–71; in Ghālib, *al-Ḥaraka al-Bāṭiniyya fī'l-Islām*, pp. 205–33, and in *Majmū'at rasā'il al-Kirmānī*, pp. 113–33.

—— *al-Aqwāl al-dhahabiyya*, ed. Ṣalāh al-Ṣāwī, Tehran 1977.

Kraus, Paul, 'Hebräische und syrische Zitate in ismā'īlitischen Schriften,' *Der Islam*, 19 (1931), pp. 243–63.

Lerner, Ralph and Muhsin Mahdi, eds, *Medieval Political Philosophy: A*

Sourcebook, Ithaca, NY, 1972.

Madelung, Wilferd, 'Das Imamat in der frühen ismailitischen Lehre,' *Der Islam,* 37 (1961), pp. 43–135.

—— 'The Assumption of the Title Shāhānshāh by the Būyids and "The Reign of the Daylam (*Dawlat al-Daylam*)",' *Journal of Near Eastern Studies,* 28 (1969), pp. 84–108 and 168–83.

al-Majdū', Ismā'īl b. 'Abd al-Rasūl, *Fihrist al-Majdū',* ed. 'Alīnaqī Mūnzavī, Tehran, 1966.

al-Maqrīzī, Taqī al-Dīn Aḥmad, *Itti'āẓ al-ḥunafā' bi-akhbār al-a'imma al-Fāṭimiyyīn al-khulafā',* vol. 1, ed. J. al-Shayyāl, Cairo, 1967, vols 2 and 3, ed. M. H. M. Aḥmad, Cairo, 1971 and 1973.

McDermott, Martin J., *The Theology of Al-Shaikh Al-Mufīd (d. 413/1022),* Beirut, 1986.

al-Nu'mān, al-Qāḍī Abū Ḥanīfa, *Da'ā'im al-Islām,* ed. A. A. A. Fyzee, Cairo, 1951–61.

Peterson, Daniel, 'Ḥamīd al-Dīn al-Kirmānī on Creation' in A. Hasnawi et al., eds, *Perspectives arabes et médiévales sur la tradition scientifique et philosophique grecque,* Louvain–Paris, 1997, pp. 555–67.

Pines, S., 'Shī'ite terms and conceptions in Judah Halevi's Kuzari,' *Jerusalem Studies in Arabic and Islam,* 2 (1980), pp. 165–251.

Poonawala, Ismail K., 'Idrīs b. al-Ḥasan,' *EI2, Supplement,* p. 407.

—— *Biobibliography of Ismā'īlī Literature,* Malibu, California, 1977.

al-Rāzī, Abū Bakr Muḥammad b. Zakariyā', *Rasā'il falsafiyya,* ed. P. Kraus, Cairo, 1939.

al-Rāzī, Abū Ḥātim Aḥmad, *A'lām al-nubuwwa,* ed. Ṣalāḥ al-Ṣāwī and G. A'wānī, Tehran, 1977.

—— *Kitāb al-iṣlāḥ,* Ms. Hamdani Collection.

Saleh, Abdel Hamid, 'Ibn Khalaf', *EI2, Supplement,* p. 390.

Sayyid, Ayman Fu'ād, 'Nuṣūṣ ḍā'i'a min Akhbār Miṣr li'l-Musabbiḥī,' *Annales Islamologiques,* 17 (1981), pp. 1–54.

al-Sijistānī, Abū Ya'qūb Isḥāq, *Ithbāt al-nubuwwa* (or *al-nubuwwāt*), ed. 'Ā. Tāmir, Beirut, 1966. Ms. Fyzee Collection.

—— *Kitāb al-iftikhār,* ed. M. Ghālib, Beirut, 1980. A definitive edition by I. K Poonawala is not yet published and, until now, is available only from the editor.

—— *Kitāb al-maqālīd,* Ms. Hamdani Collection.

—— *Kitāb al-yanābī',* ed. with partial trans. into French by H. Corbin in his *Trilogie ismaélienne,* Tehran and Paris, 1961. See also Walker, *The Wellsprings of Wisdom.*

Sourdel, D., 'al-Kādir bi'llāh,' *EI2*, vol. 4, pp. 378–9.

van Ess, Josef, 'Zur Chronologie der Werke des Ḥamīdaddīn al-Kirmānī' in 'Biobibliographische Notizen zur islamischen Theologie,' *Die Welt des Orients*, 9 (1978), pp. 255–61.

—— *Chiliastische Erwartungen und die Versuchung der Göttlichkeit: Der Kalif al-Ḥākim (386–411 H.)*, Heidelberg, 1977.

Walker, Paul E., *Abū Ya'qūb al-Sijistānī: Intellectual Missionary*, London, 1996.

—— 'The Doctrine of Metempsychosis in Islam' in *Islamic Studies Presented to Charles J. Adams*, eds W. Hallaq and D. Little, Leiden, 1991, pp. 219–38.

—— *Early Philosophical Shiism: The Ismaili Neoplatonism of Abū Ya'qūb al-Sijistānī*, Cambridge, 1993.

—— 'Fatimid Institutions of Learning,' *Journal of the American Research Center in Egypt*, 34 (1997), pp. 179–200.

—— 'The Ismaili Da'wa in the Reign of the Fatimid Caliph al-Ḥākim,' *Journal of the American Research Center in Egypt*, 30 (1993), pp. 161–82.

—— 'Platonisms in Islamic Philosophy,' *Studia Islamica*, 79 (1994), pp. 5–25.

—— [Review of] *La Quiétude de l'Intellect* by D. De Smet, *Journal of the American Oriental Society*, 117 (1997), pp. 386–7.

—— *The Wellsprings of Wisdom: A Study of Abū Ya'qūb al-Sijistānī's* Kitāb al-Yanābī', Salt Lake City, Utah, 1994.

Index

al-'Abbās b. Shu'ayb 24
Abbasids, Abbasid dynasty 2, 3, 10, 13, 14, 15, 16, 38, 39
'Abd al-Jabbār, Mu'tazilī *qāḍī* and author 16, 36, 46
'Abd al-Raḥīm b. Ilyās 7, 24
Abraham 111
Abū Ḥanīfa 55
Abū Muḥammad 126, 127
Abū Naṣr Ṣadaqa b. 'Alī al-Falāḥī, Fatimid vizier 55
Abū Shujā' Muḥammad al-Ashraf b. Muḥammad, Fatimid vizier 13
Abu'l-Faḍl Ja'far (*ālim al-'ulamā'*) 7, 24
'adāla (probity) 53
Adam 44, 63, 102, 133
'Aḍud al-Dawla, Buyid amir 8, 14
ahl al-da'wa (people of the *da'wa*) 49
ahl al-ḥaqq (people of the truth) 51
ahl al-'ibādatayn (people of double observance) 66
ahl al-ijmā' (people of consensus) 43
ahl al-istiḥsān (proponents of considering what is best) 43
ahl al-istidlāl wa'l-naẓar (proponents of inference and speculation) 43
ahl al-janna (people of paradise) 71
ahl al-qiyās (proponents of juridical analogy) 43
ahl al-ra'y wa'l-ijtihād (proponents of personal opinion and effort) 43
ahl al-taqlīd (proponents of imitation) 43
al-Akhram, Druze leader 22, 23, 42, 50, 51, 65, 66
'Alī b. Abī Ṭālib, first Shī'ī Imam 11, 16, 38, 45, 54, 106, 108
'Alī b. al-Ḥusayn b. Aḥmad al-Iṣfahānī 39
'Alī b. Mazyad 14
'amal (works) 66–7, 69, 70–1, 98, 112
amr (command of God) 71, 85, 93
Amthāl, Book of 55
angels 77, 82, 106
'aql (intellect, reason) 53, 59, 60, 83, 91, 97, 101, 102,

124; active; 91; cosmic 81; first 44, 85, 86, 87, 88, 91, 93, 94, 95, 96, 97, 102, 109, 115; hierarchy of 58; hylic (*'aql hayūlānī*) 101–2; second 91, 94, 95, 96, 97, 115; universal, first 22, 59, 60, 90, 91
al-Aqwāl al-dhahabiyya (al-Kirmānī) 29, 31, 32, 33, 35, 36, 37, 72, 73, 127, 128, 129, 130
Ārā' ahl al-madīna al-fāḍila (al-Fārābī) 120
Arabic language 55
Aristotle, Aristotelian 27, 52, 59, 90, 91, 92, 93, 102, 120
asās (founder, executor) 70, 82, 113
aṣḥāb al-adwār (masters of the ages) 102
Ash'arites 14, 43, 54
Astronomy 110
atheism 86
Avicenne et le récit visionnaire (Corbin) 124
al-azal (the eternal) 40
al-Azhar, mosque and university 39
al-'Azīz, Fatimid caliph 14, 55

bāb (gate) 113, 114
bāṭin, bāṭinī (hidden, esoteric meaning) 21, 41, 62, 63, 64, 65, 66, 67, 68, 69, 72, 73, 74, 75–6, 77, 79
Baghdad 2, 10, 11, 14, 15, 16, 31, 36
Bahā' al-Dawla, Buyid amir 11, 13
al-Bāqillānī, Mālikī Ash'arite jurist 14
body 107–8, 117
al-Bustī 26
Buyids, Buyid dynasty 3, 11, 13, 16, 36, 123
Cairo 5, 9, 10, 14, 15, 16, 17, 20, 24, 26, 31, 32, 35, 38, 43, 49, 51, 65, 66, 73, 123
Christians, Christianity 90
Church of the Holy Sepulchre (Jerusalem) 8
city, concept of 45
command *see amr*
Corbin, Henry 124
cosmic intellect *see 'aql*
cosmology 22, 78, 82, 89, 90, 91, 94, 96–8; early Ismaili 27, 58, 90, 93–4; of al-Kirmani 89–103; Neoplatonic 22, 91
creation 50, 53, 58, 78, 80, 81, 84, 85, 87, 89, 92, 93, 94, 95, 99, 105, 108, 116, 117

Da'ā'im al-Islām (al-Qāḍī al-Nu'mān) 56, 69
dā'ī (missionary) 1, 2, 3, 4, 5, 16, 18, 21, 22, 23, 26, 27, 28, 39, 40, 42, 43, 44, 45, 46, 47, 48, 49, 50, 51, 52, 56, 57, 60, 69, 72, 78, 82, 84, 89, 90, 98, 113, 114, 118, 123, 124
dā'ī al-du'āt (chief *dā'ī*) 4, 9, 39
dā'ī muṭlaq (*dā'ī* with absolute authority) 114
Damascus 8
Dār al-'Ilm (House of Knowledge) in Cairo 7
al-Darazī, Muḥammad b. Ismā'īl, Druze leader 22, 23, 65
da'wa (mission, religio-political

propaganda) 2, 3, 4–11 *passim,* 14–23 *passim,* 25–46 *passim,* 47, 48–51, 52–9 *passim,* 60–1, 62–8 *passim,* 72–6 *passim,* 77–9; 85–92 *passim,* 104, 105, 112–16, 118, 119, 124, 131, 132
Day of Resurrection *see qiyāma*
Daysān 111
De Smet, Daniel 120, 131
double observance *see 'ibāda*
double worship (double observance) 20
Druze 24

Egypt 3, 4, 7, 8, 9, 13, 14, 16, 17, 20, 21, 22, 23, 24, 25, 31, 32, 33, 34, 38, 39, 40, 41, 42, 45, 46, 65, 123, 132
emanation (*fayḍ*) 53, 109
Enneads (Plotinus) 59, 90, 106
executor (*waṣī, awṣiyā'*) 69, 77, 81, 82, 91, 106, 112

Fakhr al-Mulk, Abū Ghālib 'Alī b. Muḥammad b. Khalaf, Buyid vizier 11, 13, 14, 15, 16, 31
al-Fārābī, Abū Naṣr, philosopher 27, 52, 89, 90, 91, 92, 94, 96, 101, 119, 120, 121, 122, 124
al-Fāriqī, Ismaili jurist and *dā'ī* 5, 6, 7, 17
Fārs, Persia 10, 11
Fatḥ, angel 58
Fatimids, Fatimid dynasty 1, 3, 4, 5, 8, 9, 13, 14, 16, 21, 35, 41, 59, 61, 64, 69, 72, 123
first intellect see *'aql*
first processive (*inbi'āthī*) being 97
form (*ṣūra*) 83, 95
Fustat 5, 11, 22

Gabriel (Jibrā'īl), angel 113
Ghulāt (exaggerators in religion) 21, 35, 43, 52, 63, 67
Gospels 55
Greek 52, 90
Gurjānj 122

al-Ḥadā'iq (al-Kirmānī) 130
ḥadīth 70, 106, 108
al-Ḥākim bi-Amr Allāh, Fatimid caliph 1, 2, 3, 4, 5, 6, 7, 8, 9, 11, 12, 13, 14, 15, 16, 18, 19, 20, 21, 22, 24, 30, 31, 38, 39, 42, 45, 47, 49, 56, 63, 65, 89, 90, 118, 127
Hamadān, Persia 122
Ḥamza, Druze leader 22, 23, 65
Ḥanbalī school, Ḥanbalīs 7
hayūlā (prime matter) 44, 83, 95, 98, 99, 135, 136
Ḥayy ibn Yaqẓān 124
Hebrew language 55
hell 110
hierarchies *see ḥudūd*
ḥikma (wisdom) 53
al-Ḥilla 14
History (Yaḥyā of Antioch) 3
ḥudūd (hierarchies) 76, 83, 113
ḥujja (proof) 10, 46, 50, 60, 113, 114
al-ḥukamā (scholars) 98

al-Īḍāḥ (al-Qāḍī al-Nu'mān) 56
'ibāda (observance, veneration) 20, 41, 66, 67, 69
'ibāda al-'amaliyya (practical service) 66, 77
'ibāda al-'ilmiyya (knowledge by

observance) 74, 80, 81
ibādatayn (double observance) 32, 41, 48, 62, 66, 68, 69, 71, 72, 76, 80, 106, 112, 113, 116
ibdā', *ibdā'ī* (origination, innovation, creation) 50, 83, 92, 93, 95, 101, 102, 109
Ibn 'Abbās 55
Ibn Abi'l-'Awwām, Fatimid judge 7, 24
Ibn Durayd 55
Ibn al-Muqanna' 111
Ibn Sīnā, Abū 'Alī Husayn (Avicenna) 3, 27, 59, 89, 94, 122, 123, 124
Ibn Tufayl 124
Idrīs 'Imād al-Dīn, Ṭayyibī historian 3, 4, 10, 28, 29, 30, 125, 126, 127, 128, 129, 130
'iffa (purity) 43, 53, 58, 76
Iklīl al-nafs wa tājuhā (al-Kirmānī) 29, 32, 35, 37, 130
'ilm (knowledge) 45, 62, 66, 67, 69, 70, 72, 74, 80, 81; *'ilm ta'līmī*, (knowledge by instruction) 109
imams, imamate 2, 18, 19, 20, 21, 22, 23, 24, 37, 42, 43, 45, 49, 54, 60, 62, 63, 69, 76, 77, 78, 81, 82, 88, 92, 102, 106, 113, 114, 115, 118, 121, 122, 124
inbi'āth (emanation) 95, 101, 102 *see also* emanation
innovation *see ibdā'*
Innovator (*mubdi'*) 92
instruction *see ta'līm*
intellect *see 'aql*
Iqlīmas (Simeon the Pure) 56
al-Iqtiṣār (al-Qāḍī al-Nu'mān) 56
Iraq 3, 10, 11, 13, 14, 15, 16, 18, 23, 24, 26, 31, 32, 33, 34, 36, 38, 45, 47
Isḥāqiyya 43
al-Iṣlāḥ (Abū Ḥātim al-Rāzī) 57, 60
Iṣfahān, Persia 122
Isrāfīl (Seraphiel), angel 113
al-Iṣṭakhrī 15
Ithnā 'ashariyya see Twelvers

Jadd, angel 58
Ja'far b. Manṣūr al-Yaman 56
al-Jāḥiẓ 38, 46
Ja'far al-Ṣādiq, Shī'ī imam 8, 64, 71
Jamhara (Ibn Durayd) 55
al-Jarājikī 26
jazīra (region, Ismaili diocese) 46
Jesus 102, 109, 111
Jews 55
jihād 12, 43, 69, 74, 75, 78, 115
Jīlān, Persia 49
Jīruft, Kirmān, Persia 11, 49
Jupiter 97
Jurjān, Persia 122

Ka'ba 96
al-Kalbī 55
kalima (Word of God) 62, 85, 93
Khalīl b. Aḥmad 55
Khatkīn, Abū Manṣūr (al-'Aḍudī), chief *dā'ī* 8, 9, 18, 23, 28, 31, 39, 46, 113
Khayāl, angel 58
al-Khazā'in fī funūn al-'ilm wa'l-ta'wīl 29
Khurasan, Persia 122, 123
Kirmān, Persia 11

al-Kirmānī, Ḥamīd al-Dīn 3, 4, cosmology 80–3, 89–98; on the *da'wa* 48, 50–1; doctrine of soul 99–103, double observance 20–1, 48, 66–79, 80; in Egypt 8–9, 16–24, 41–4; and Ghulāt 21–4, 42; on the imamate 18–20; in Iraq 10–16; and Mu'tazila 51–2; and Philosophers 51–3, 89; the *Rāḥat al-'aql* 104–17; sources 54–61; on *ta'līm* 76–9; on *tawḥīd* 83–9; works 25–46; on the *ẓāhir* and *bāṭin* 66–76
Kitāb al-'aqā'id wa' lubāb al-fawā'id 29
Kitāb al-'ayn (Khalīl b. Aḥmad) 55
Kitāb al-ḥiyal (Abū Ḥanīfa) 55
Kitāb al-maghāzī (al-Qāḍī al-Nu'mān) 56
Kitāb al-maqālīd (al-Sijistānī) 40
Kitāb al-muqāyis (al-Kirmānī) 29
Kitāb maydān al-'uqūl (al-Kirmānī) 29
Kitāb al-naqd wa'l-ilzām (al-Kirmānī) 29
Kitāb al-ṭahāra (al-Qāḍī al-Nu'mān) 56
Kitāb ta'wīl al-sharī'a (al-Mu'izz) 56
Kitāb al-'Uthmāniyya (al-Jāḥiẓ) 38
knowledge *see 'ilm*

Last Day 82
lawḥ (tablet) 58, 94, 98, 113
law 5, 7, 55, 64, 77, 78–9, 63, 64, 66, 67, 68, 69, 71, 73, 75, 77, 78–9, 82, 96, 97, 108, 111, 112, 113, 116, 122, 131, 135; *qānūn* 109, 110, 111 *see also sharī'a*
legislator, lawgiver (*shāri'*) 108–9, 112, 113, 121, 122
logic 120

Ma'āṣim al-hudā (al-Kirmānī) 29, 30, 31, 36, 38, 128
ma'dhūn 49
ma'dhūn maḥṣūr 114
ma'dhūn muṭlaq 114
Madina 8, 11
al-Mafāwiz wa'l-ḥadā'iq (al-Kirmānī) 32, 35, 130
al-Maṣābīḥ fī ithbāt al-imāma (al-Kirmānī) 11, 29, 31, 33, 36, 37, 49, 57, 126, 127, 128
al-Mahdī (Fatimid caliph) 20
Maḥmūd of Ghazna, Ghaznawid sultan 13, 39
al-Maḥṣūl (al-Nasafī) 44, 57, 60, 61, 85
al-Majālis al-Baghdādiyya wa'l-Baṣriyya (al-Kirmānī) 10, 29, 35, 130
majālis al-ḥikma (sessions of wisdom) 4, 5, 6, 7, 8, 16, 17
al-Majdū', Ismā'īl b. 'Abd al-Rasūl, Dā'ūdī author 126, 127, 128
Mālikī Sunnism 14
al-Manāqib wa'l-mathālib (al-Qāḍī al-Nu'mān) 56
al-Manṣūr, Fatimid caliph 19
Mars 97
Maydān al-'aql (al-Kirmānī) 36, 130
Mazyadids 14
Mercury 97
messiah (*mahdī*) 64, 111, 117
metaphysics 27, 82
metempsychosis (*tanāsukh*) 36

Michael 113
mīzān al-diyāna (balance of religion) 114, 131
al-Mu'ayyad bi'llāh Aḥmad b. al-Ḥusayn, Zaydī imam 38
mubdi' (innovator) 92, 93
al-Mufīd, Shaykh 15, 16
Muḥammad b. Ismā'īl 64
Muḥammad, the Prophet 1, 15, 16, 21, 38, 39, 45, 53, 54, 55, 62, 64, 69, 73, 77, 78, 79, 106, 108, 110, 111, 115
al-Mu'izz, Fatimid caliph 19, 20, 56
mukāsir 114
Mukhtaṣar al-āthār (al-Qāḍī al-Nu'mān) 56
al-Muqāyis (al-Kirmānī) 32, 35, 37
al-Murshid, Abū 'Īsā 58
al-Musabbiḥī, Muḥammad b. 'Ubayd Allah, historian 3, 8
al-Mustanṣir, Fatimid caliph 13, 24, 27
Mu'tazilīs, Mu'tazilism 15, 16, 36, 43, 52, 53, 54, 84

nafs see soul
al-Naqd wa'l-ilzām (al-Kirmānī) 16, 32, 35, 36, 130
al-Nasafī, Muḥammad b. Aḥmad (al-Nakhshabī), Ismaili *dā'ī* and author 44, 45, 50, 56, 57, 59, 61, 72, 84, 85, 89, 118
Nāṣir Khusraw, Ismaili *dā'ī* and author 27, 89
naṣṣ (designation) 54
nāṭiq (speaking-prophet) 34, 60, 70
Neoplatonism 22, 27, 58, 59, 90, 91, 94, 92, 95, 98, 123, 124
Noah 111
al-Nu'mān b. Muḥammad, al-Qaḍī Abū Ḥanīfa, Ismaili jurist and author 5, 26, 56, 69, 72
Nuṣayriyya ('Alawīs) 43

paradise 110
Peter 56
Philosophers (*al-falāsifa*) 42, 43, 51, 52, 53, 54, 63, 64, 67, 74, 82, 84, 86, 88, 91, 92, 93, 94, 96, 97, 98, 118, 119, 134, 141
pilgrimage 43, 63, 69, 74, 75
Plato 90, 120
Plotinus 59, 90, 92, 106
prophets, prophecy 77, 79, 82, 91, 106, 109, 110

al-qaḍā' 44
al-qadar 44
al-Qāḍī al-Nu'mān *see* al-Nu'mān b. Muḥammad
qāḍī al-quḍāt (chief *qāḍī*) 4
al-Qādir, Abbasid caliph 13, 14, 39
al-Qā'im bi-Amr Allāh, Fatimid caliph 56
qalam (Pen) 58, 94, 98, 113
Qarmatian 64
Qirwash b. al-Muqallad 14
qiyāma (Day of Resurrection) 70, 82, 140
La Quiétude de l'intellect (De Smet) 131
Qur'ān 33, 62, 70, 83, 86, 87, 109

Rāḥat al-'aql (al-Kirmānī) 10, 23, 24, 29, 30, 32, 33, 34, 36,

43, 44, 45, 46, 52, 56, 72, 104–6, 114, 124, 125, 126, 127, 128, 129, 130, 131, 132
Rayy, Persia 36, 122
al-Rāzī, Abū Bakr 37, 45, 55, 73, 74, 119
al-Rāzī, Abū Ḥātim, Ismaili *dāʿī* and author 37, 43, 44, 56, 57, 60, 61, 72
resurrection *see qiyāma*
revelation 110, 111
reward 82
al-Risāla al-durriyya (al-Kirmānī) 9, 31, 32, 33, 39, 40, 126
Risālat al-fihrist (al-Kirmānī) 29, 33, 129
al-Risāla al-ḥāwiya (al-Kirmānī) 30, 31, 32, 33, 34, 40, 127
al-Risāla al-kāfiya (al-Kirmānī) 32, 38, 40, 72, 127
al-Risāla al-layliyya (al-Kirmānī) 129
al-Risāla al-lāzima (al-Kirmānī) 31, 34, 35, 40, 126, 126
al-Risāla al-muḍīʾa (al-Kirmānī) 29, 31, 32, 33, 40, 41, 126
al-Risāla al-raḍiyya (al-Kirmānī) 31, 32, 40, 126
al-Risāla al-rawḍa (al-Kirmānī) 32, 33, 40, 126
al-Risāla al-taʾwīliyya (al-Kirmānī) 29, 130,
al-Risāla al-wāʿiẓa (al-Kirmānī) 30, 40, 42, 50, 127
al-Risāla al-zāhira (al-Kirmānī) 127
Risālat mabāsim al-bishārāt (al-Kirmānī) 9, 22, 30, 31, 32, 38, 39, 40 127
Risālat al-mafāwiz waʾl-ḥadāʾiq (al-Kirmānī) 29
Risālat al-nuẓum (al-Kirmānī) 29, 31, 32, 40, 126
al-Riyāḍ (al-Kirmānī) 32, 33, 43, 44, 45, 57, 58, 59, 60, 76, 85, 98, 126, 127, 128, 129, 130
al-sābiq (preceder) 58, 94
salvation 11
Saturn 97
scripture 113
second procession (*al-munbaʿith al-thānī*) 98, 116
secondary beings (*al-thawānī*) 74
second creation 116 *see also* creation
secondary effect (*mafʿūl*) 95
Sharḥ al-akhbār (al-Qāḍī al-Nuʿmān) 56
sharīʿa 43, 56, 57, 64, 69, 109, 112
Sharīf al-Murtaḍā 11
Shīʿīs, Shīʿism 8, 11, 13, 14, 15, 16, 21, 38, 42, 52, 63, 64, 72, 121, 122
Shīrāz, Persia 27, 49
al-Shiʿrī fiʾl-khawāṣṣ (al-Kirmānī) 30, 33, 129
Shukūk ʿalā jālīnūs (Abū Bakr al-Rāzī) 55
al-Sijistānī, Abū Yaʿqūb, Ismaili *dāʿī* and author 27, 40, 41, 43, 44, 45, 50, 51, 56, 57, 58, 59, 61, 68, 72, 84, 85, 87, 89, 90, 91, 92, 93, 98, 118, 123, 124
Simeon the Pure 56
Sīra (Biography of the Prophet) 32, 40, 55
al-Siyāsa al-madaniyya (al-Fārābī) 120
soul (*nafs*) 36, 44, 59, 60, 76, 78, 81, 83, 91, 98, 99, 100,

101, 102, 103, 107–8, 111, 112, 116, 117; universal 22, 44, 59, 90, 91, 94, 95, 98, 124
Sufis, Sufism 42, 63, 64
Sunni Islam, Sunnis 15, 16, 35
Syria 8, 28
Syriac language 55

Ṭabaristān, Persia 49
Taḥṣīl al-sa'āda (al-Fārābī) 120, 121
al-Ṭa'i', Abbasid caliph 13
Tāj al-'uqūl (al-Kirmānī) 29, 32, 35, 129
al-tālī (the follower) 58
ta'līm (instruction) 49–50, 54, 76–9, 81, 109 *see also* teacher
Tanbīh al-hādī wa'l-mustahdī (al-Kirmānī) 29, 32, 33, 42, 48, 52, 57, 128
tanzīl (revelation) 62, 63, 77
taqiyya (dissimulation) 124
tawḥīd (oneness of God) 9, 39, 44, 61, 76, 68, 77, 82, 83, 84–9, 106, 126, 128
al-Tawḥīd (al-Kirmānī) 130
ta'wīl (esoteric interpretation) 21, 29, 33, 43, 56, 62, 63, 69, 72, 79, 113, 128, 130
Ta'wīl al-sharī'a (al-Mu'izz) 56
Ṭayyibīs, Ṭayyibiyya, Ismaili community 10, 25, 27, 28, 44
teacher, instructor 49, 53, 54, 76, 77, 78, 79, 83, 88, 92, 101, 102, 108, 111, 112, 125, 132
Theologia (Plotinus) 90
Theology (Aristotle) 59
al-Ṭibb al-rūḥānī (Abū Bakr al-Rāzī) 37
Torah 55
Twelvers, Twelver Shī'ism 3, 11, 14, 15, 26, 43, 54

'Umar b. al-Khaṭṭāb, second caliph 38
universal intellect *see 'aql*
universal soul *see nafs*
unmoved mover 84, 89, 91, 93
'Uthmān b. 'Affān, third caliph 38
'Uyūn al-akhbār (Idrīs 'Imād al-Dīn) 3, 28

Venus 97

al-Waḍī'a fī ma'ālim al-dīn (al-Kirmānī) 11, 22, 24, 29, 32, 33, 37, 41, 42, 56, 57, 68, 72, 74, 78, 80
waḥda (oneness of God) 47, 49, 53, 72, 74, 77, 93, 105, 133, 134
al-Waḥīda fi'l-ma'ād (al-Kirmānī) 29, 32, 35, 57, 129
wājib al-wujūd (necessary being) 86, 91
will (*irāda*) 93

Yaḥyā of Antioch, historian 3, 8, 9
Ya'qūb b. Killis, Fatimid vizier 55
Yemen 28, 29, 30, 129, 130

ẓāhir, ẓāhiri 41, 63, 65, 66, 67, 68, 69, 72, 75, 79
al-Zāhira (al-Kirmānī) 32, 40
Zaydīs, Zaydīyya, Shī'ī community 13, 26, 43, 53, 73, 74, 75